AMARNA

THE MISSING EVIDENCE

SUE MOSELEY

Peach Pixel

The lives of people living in Ancient Egypt has fascinated readers for generations, and the most intriguing events surround the royal families of the 18th dynasty, in the 1300s BC. Traditions were broken at the end of the dynasty, with the arrival of a strange Pharaoh, Akhenaten. This Pharaoh was different. His art was most unusual. Was he really a woman? Did he suffer from an unknown disease that explained his strange elongated shape, his breasts, prominent hips and belly?

For almost 200 years there has been continued speculation about the identity of Pharaoh Smenkhkare, the enigmatic successor to Akhenaten --- known as the Heretic. Was Smenkhkare an unknown son of Akhenaten? Was he his brother? Or was he a new lover who came onto the scene at the death of Nefertiti?

The evidence has always existed which explains the succession, but has been ignored until now.
Where was Akhenaten buried? Was Tutankhamen murdered by an ambitious rival for the crown of Egypt?

Amarna --- the Missing evidence gives the answers to these mysteries, and provides a new understanding of the lives of the royal family.

Sue Moseley uses a combination of new evidence and a re-interpretation of established facts to bring a new and exciting book which not only makes sense of a confusing period of history but challenges the reader to join in by solving puzzles and adding their own contributions via social networking.

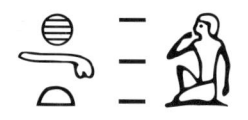

Published by Peach Pixel
5 Solent View, Calshot, Hampshire, SO45 1BH

First published 2009

Copyright © Sue Moseley 2009
The moral right of the author has been asserted.
All rights reserved.

The author and publisher gratefully acknowledge the permission granted to reproduce the copyrighted material in this book.

Without limiting the rights under copyright reserved above, no part of this publication may be reproduced, stored in or introduced into a retrieval system, or transmitted, in any form, or by any means (electronic, mechanical, photocopying, recording or otherwise) without the prior written permission of the copyright owner and the above publisher of this book.

Every effort has been made to trace copyright holders and to obtain their permission for the use of copyright material. The author and publisher apologise for any errors or omissions in the above list and would be grateful if they could be notified of any corrections that should be incorporated in future reprints or editions of this book.

Printed by Hobbs the Printers Limited
Registered Office: Brunel Road, Totton, Hampshire, SO40 3WX

ISBN: 978-0-9561693-0-3

For Richard, Benjamin and Abigail

Contents

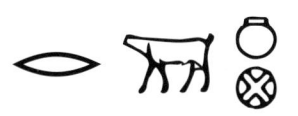

List of illustrations.		ix
Acknowledgements.		xv
Introduction, and How to Read this Book		2
Chapter 1	The Story so far ---	8
Chapter 2	The Founding of Akhetaten.	34
Chapter 3	Who lived at Akhetaten?	60
Chapter 4	Art at Akhetaten.	78
Chapter 5	The Co-Regency.	92
Chapter 6	Years 3, 6, 9 and 12.	108
Chapter 7	The Elusive Smenkhkare.	130
Chapter 8	Nefertiti, Pharaoh of Egypt.	156
Chapter 9	The Aftermath.	180
Chapter 10	Tutankhamen and Aye.	200
Conclusion.		214
Revised Timeline		218
Further Reading		220
Index.		224

List of Illustrations

Chapter 1

1.1 Pharaoh Amenhotep I with his mother queen Ahmose-Nefertari. 18th dynasty of Egypt. Scan from old book Culturgeschichte by K. Faulmann (1881)

1.2 Amenhotep I from the tomb of Ahmose Nefertari. Scan from Report on some excavations in the Theban necropolis during the winter of 1889. The Marquis of Northampton.

1.3 Replica of the Abydos Kings' List at the British Museum. Photo: Author's own.

1.4 Statue of Tuthmoses III. National Museum Cairo. Photo: Author's own.

1.5 Statue of Hatshepsut. Metropolitan Museum of Art, New York.

1.6 Statue of Tuthmoses IV and his mother Tiaa. National Museum Cairo. Photo: Author's own.

1.7 The Dream Stelae. Giza. Photo: Author's own.

1.8 Scene from tomb 226 Valley of the Nobles, showing a very young Amenhotep III with his mother Mutemwia. Norman and Nina de Garis Davies.

1.9 Statue of Amenhotep IV/Akhenaten. National Museum Cairo. Photo: Author's own.

1.10 Fragment showing the royal couple with three of their children. Egyptian Museum Berlin.

Chapter 2

2.1 The marriage scarab. From "Amarna Age. A study of the Crisis of the Ancient World." Rev. James Baikie 1926

2.2. Prince Tuthmoses on his bier. National Museum Cairo. Photo: Author's own.

2.3 This colossal statue is Amenhotep III, Queen Tiy and their three daughters. National Museum Cairo. Photo: Author's own.

2.4 The site of the city of Akhetaten today. A barren, desert site. Photo Author's own.

2.5. Boundary Stelae U Photo: Author's own.

2.6 Boundary Stelae A. Photo: Author's own.

2.7 The Weighing of the Heart ceremony from the Book of the Dead.

2.8 Plan of Akhetaten.

2.9. Mud bricks at Akhetaten. Photo: Author's own.

Chapter 3

3.1 Scene from Ahmose's tomb. Photo: Authors own.

3.2 . Scene from Meryre I's tomb. Photo: Author's own.

3.3. Pentu rewarded with Gold Collars.

3.4 Scene from Penhesy's tomb. Photo: Authors own.

3.5 Parennefer rewarded with Gold Collars.

3.6 Tutu rewarded with Gold Collars.

3.7 Scene of worship from Tutu's tomb.

3.8 Scene of worship from Mahu's tomb.

3.9 Scene from the Amarna tomb of Aye showing Aye and his wife Tiy receiving gifts from Akhenaten, Nefertiti, Merytaten and Ankhesenpaaten.

3.10. Huya rewarded with Gold Collars.

Note: Apart from the Author's own photos, the illustrations in this chapter are taken from "The Rock Tombs of Tel El Amarna" by Norman de Garis Davies

Chapter 4

4.1 Statue of Akhenaten showing the elongated skull and breasts. National Museum Cairo. Photo: Author's own.

4.2 Sketch of Pablo Picasso. Self-Portrait. 1972.

4.3 Limestone stelae showing a devoted royal family. National Museum Cairo. Photo: Author's own.

4.4 Amarna head shapes. Photo: Andrew Jones

4.5 Akhenaten in the 9th year of his reign, with Nefertiti. Louvre Museum, Paris. Photo: Author's own.

4.6 Head of Nefertiti from **4.5** above.

4.7 Heads of Akhenaten and Nefertiti. Brooklyn Museum of Art. New York. Photo: Andrew Jones

Chapter 5

5.1 An Amarna letter. Louvre Museum, Paris..Photo: Author's own.

5.2 Amarna Letter EA27. From "Amarna Age. A study of the Crisis of the Ancient World." Rev. James Baikie 1926

5.3 Wall painting showing the four prophets of Amun from tomb 55 in the Valley of the Nobles. Norman de Garis Davies.

5.4 The scene of grief from the Royal tomb. Norman de Garis Davies.

5.5 Scene from Huya's tomb showing Akhenaten and his family on the left and Amenhotep III, Tiy and Beketaten on the right. Norman de Garis Davies.

5.6 Scene of Foreign Tribute. Tomb of Huya. Norman de Garis Davies.

5.7 Scene of Foreign Tribute. Tomb of Meryre II. Norman de Garis Davies.

5.8 Cartouches of Akhenaten followed by Amenhotep III.

Chapter 6

6.1 Map of the Tombs.

6.2 The Early and Late names of the Aten.

6.3 The Aten Names from Battiscombe Gunn.

6.4 Akhenaten leading his mother, Queen Tiy. Scene from Huya's tomb. "The Rock Tombs of Tel El Amarna" by Norman de Garis Davies

6.5 The inscriptions showing the later names of the Aten and Neb-maat-re.

6.6 Scene showing Amenhotep III from Huya's tomb. "The Rock Tombs of Tel El Amarna" by Norman de Garis Davies

6.7 Akhenaten and Nefertiti entertain Queen Tiy and Beketaten. From Huya's tomb. "The Rock Tombs of Tel El Amarna" by Norman de Garis Davies

6.8 Scenes of grief over the death of Meketaten. From the Royal Tomb. "The Rock Tombs of Tel El Amarna" by Norman de Garis Davies

Chapter 7

7.1 Gurob Ring

7.2 Petrie's Rings. Petrie, W.M.Flinders. Tell El Amarna. 1894

7.3 Ankheperure rings from Amarna. Petrie, W.M.Flinders. Tell El Amarna. 1894

7.4 Newberry's cartouches.

7.5 The erased cartouches. "The Rock Tombs of Tel El Amarna" by Norman de Garis Davies

7.6 Robert Hay's original work. Courtesy the British Library.

7.7 A clearer view of Robert Hay's work.

7.8 Lepsius Original squeeze. Courtesy Berlin-Brandenburgian Academy of the Sciences

7.9 Lepsius cartouches in the correct order.

7.10 The scene from the North Wall of the tomb of Meryre II. "The Rock Tombs of Tel El Amarna" by Norman de Garis Davies

7.11 The North wall of the Tomb of Meryre II today. Photo: Bob Hanawalt.

Chapter 8

1 Mutnodjme and her nieces. "The Rock Tombs of Tel El Amarna" by Norman de Garis Davies

8.2 Ramases The Great with his Great Royal Wife Nefertari standing by his right knee. Abu Simbul. Photo: Author's own.

8.3 The Kissing statue. National Museum Cairo. Photo: Author's own.

8.4 Ring showing Akhenaten and Nefertiti as Shu and Tefnut. Amarna.

8.5 Akhenaten and Nefertiti as Shu and Tefnut.. "The Rock Tombs of Tel El Amarna" by Norman de Garis Davies

8.6 Nefertiti wearing the Atef crown. "The Rock Tombs of Tel El Amarna" by Norman de Garis Davies

8.7 Some more of Petrie's rings. Petrie, W.M.Flinders. Tell El Amarna. 1894

8.8 Pharaoh Nefertiti on a royal barge "smiting the enemy"

8.9 The two Amarna Pharaohs. Egyptian Museum, Berlin. Photo: Andrew Jones.

8.10 Pharaohs in love. Egyptian Museum, Berlin. Photo: Andrew Jones.

8.11 Nefertiti bust at the Berlin Museum.

Chapter 9

9.1 George VI and Elizabeth II post boxes. Photos: Author's own.

9.2 Plan of the Royal Tomb at Akhetaten.

9.3 Chamber Alpha. "The Rock Tombs of Tel El Amarna" by Norman de Garis Davies

9.4 Chamber Gamma. Normanl de Garis-Davies Rock Tombs of Tel El Amarna

9.5 The Anubis Statue from the "Tomb of Tutankhamen." Howard Carter.

9.6 The Palette between Anubis' paws from the "Tomb of Tutankhamen." Howard Carter.

9.7 The inscription on the Palette.

9.8 The nurse leaving Chamber Alpha, carrying a royal baby. "The Rock Tombs of Tel El Amarna" by Norman de Garis Davies

9.9 Close up of the inscription.

9.10 Fragment found at Ugarti showing the marriage of King Niqmat to an Amarna Princess.

9.11 The gold coffin from KV55

9.12 The canopic jars found in tomb KV55

Chapter 10

10.1 Tutankhamen's Restoration Stelae. National Museum Cairo. Photo: Author's own.

10.2 The x-ray of Tutankhamen's skull.

10.3 Aye performing the Opening of the mouth ceremony in the tomb of Tutankhamen.

10.4 The coffins and mummified remains of Tutankhamen's two daughters

Acknowledgements

I would like to offer my thanks to the many people who have helped me so much over the past years. I could not have written this book without them.

So, my thanks go first to my husband, Mike, who has helped me with the illustrations, web sites and marketing – and for putting up with me whilst writing the book.

A great many thanks go to my friend and proof reader Cath Potten, for her patient work and encouragement.

My thanks go to the British Library for its help, and the Petrie Museum who assisted in the identification of specific information about the work of the great Flinders Petrie. They go to Lucia Gahlin who helped me obtain my first Reader's Ticket at the British Library. Also to the Egypt Exploration Society for its kind permission to reproduce the works of Norman de Garis Davies.

I would also like to express my gratitude to my friend and mentor the late Bill Murnane, who persuaded me to undertake this research, and to Bob Hanawalt of the Amarna Research Foundation for his encouragement and help with the photography inside the tomb of Meryre II.

I am very grateful to Barry Kemp, Director of the Amarna project, for opening up the tomb of Meryre II and the Royal Tomb during my visit.

My thanks also go to Dr. Ingelore Hafemann from the Berlin-Brandenburgian Academy of the Sciences for her very kind help in emailing the work of Karl Lepsius, and to Dr. Sayed Hassan, Museum Director of the Cairo Museum for his generous help with photography.

Amarna --- the missing evidence

Introduction

Introduction, and how to read this book.

"Twenty years from now you will be more disappointed by the things that you didn't do than by the ones you did do. So throw off the bowlines. Sail away from the safe harbor. Catch the trade winds in your sails. Explore. Dream. Discover." -- **Mark Twain**

Front cover: painted relief showing an unnamed Pharaoh and his wife. Eighteenth Dynasty."

The picture I chose for the front cover is really important in understanding this book. It is a painted relief with no names, yet if you come across this image on the web or in other books you will be told it is a representation of Smenkhkare – the mysterious successor to Pharaoh Akhenaten, and his wife, Merytaten.

Eight years ago, when I first started my research, my mind was clearly focussed on the Pharaoh Smenkhkare, this enigmatic ruler of Ancient Egypt. I had read so much about him, but found it hard to accept what the books were telling me. I could not satisfy myself that the evidence presented, or its interpretation was reliable, and it seemed wrong to weave an important event in history around this information. I was shown images of Smenkhkare, yet nowhere was his name mentioned. I was shown evidence of his name written in tombs and on artefacts, yet when I actually studied them, his name was not there. I was hooked!

Amarna --- the missing evidence

I decided to examine every piece of so called evidence relating to Smenkhkare and see if I could make any sense of my findings. This took a long time, but with help from many wonderful people I have met throughout the journey, that work is now completed.

As with any research, one piece of information leads to another and before I knew it I was taking a fresh look at the lives of the people who must have known this Smenkhkare – Akhenaten himself, Nefertiti, Tutankhamen, Aye, Horemheb to name just a few. I found myself looking at the evidence usually presented and asking myself if we really had the full story. Some pieces did not fit. So my research into the Pharaoh Smenkhkare which should have taken no more than two years has widened into research into the lives of the Pharaohs who lived at the end of the 18th Dynasty, and the people who featured significantly in their lives.

My next problem was how to present my findings to you, the reader. A book full of facts and figures could become boring, yet I felt it would be of interest to anyone interested in Ancient Egypt. I had been interested enough to launch out on an eight year journey of detection, so my book is presented in such a way that you can decide for yourself if my findings are sound.

As I worked on my research I met a great many people who had their own ideas about what happened during what has become known as the "Amarna Period" and I wanted to create an environment where these views can be aired and added to the vast pool of information. One book cannot possibly include everything worth saying A web site has been created to run alongside this book where you, the reader can add your own information, discuss ideas and issues with others sharing the same interests, and check up on the latest findings or events.

For further information visit: www.suemoseley.com

Introduction

This is partly a critical analysis of the evidence so far presented. I have taken a holistic approach to my research rather than taking each piece in isolation. Psychology is the study of human behaviour, and this is just as important in interpreting evidence as the evidence itself. People behave in predictable ways, and this must be considered. We cannot just look at bare "facts."

From Chapter Two onwards, I have concluded by presenting two versions of events as they relate to a particular character, an event or even a period of time. I have summarised my findings and presented them alongside a summary of events as we have known them. You the reader can then decide. To add to the interest a few other challenges have been included to help you.

You will be looking at events taking place in Egypt around 1350BC, and also at International diplomacy. You can read the history of the period as printed in popular books and other publications since Amarna was first discovered by Egyptologists back in the early 1800s. In essence this version has remained unchanged over the years. I will then be offering you another version based on my years of research. You will see the research for yourself and make up your own mind.

This is not just a re-hash of old evidence, though. As I said at the beginning, my real interest was in the Pharaoh Smenkhkare who succeeded Akhenaten. Much of the evidence in Chapter Seven has never before been published.

Finally, I must apologise for the quality of some of the illustrations. I am not a professional photographer, so my photographs will not win prizes. Other illustrations are from very old documents and I have reproduced them to the best of my ability.

Amarna --- the missing evidence

So sit back and enjoy. My web site will be live from the date of publication of this book and a blog has been created for your comments.

Sue Mosley

Ancient Egypt Researcher and Author.

February 2009

The Author outside the Tomb of Meryre II at Amarna, April 2008

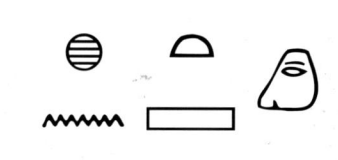

Chapter 1

The Story so far

"There is no moment of delight in any pilgrimage like the beginning of it."
-- **Charles Dudley Warner**

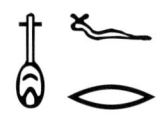

Akhenaten. Pharaoh of Egypt in the middle of the 14th century BC. His name is as well known as Ramses II and Cleopatra, but there the similarity ends. Ramses and Cleopatra are known to us from the well preserved and plentiful monuments and inscriptions they left behind; *well preserved and plentiful*; it has been easy for us to recreate their lives, their triumphs and disasters. Akhenaten left very little behind, and much of what was left has since been destroyed by natural decay or stolen by antiquities thieves.

The wonders of Ancient Egypt had been buried in sand for centuries when Napoleon's forces invaded Egypt in 1798. His invasion forces included scholars who not only investigated the great pyramids, but also travelled throughout Egypt making very scholarly reports on many of Egypt's monuments. The Rosetta Stone (1) was discovered in 1799, and by 1822 Jean-François Champollion had deciphered the hieroglyphs. The names of Ramases II and Cleopatra were introduced to Europeans and they became known to a new generation of Egyptians as well. Yet no-one knew of Akhenaten.

It was not until 1824 that John Gardner Wilkinson stumbled upon a remote, desert area of Egypt inhabited by local Egyptians and known to them as Et Til el Amarna.

Amarna --- the missing evidence

The modern town was built on what was once the city created by Pharaoh Akhenaten on the east of the Nile, about half way between the two ancient capitals of Egypt, Memphis and Thebes. The area is not very welcoming, the city having been built on a flat, desert area overlooked by vast, inhospitable cliffs.

Wilkinson travelled extensively through Egypt, but in 1826 he returned to this desert area and entered some of the tombs of the nobles; but still the name of Akhenaten was unknown. The tombs at Amarna were carved out of poor quality limestone and had been deteriorating for centuries, but once opened to the world the decay became worse and was followed by thieves on the lookout for antiquities to sell in the markets of Cairo.

As the knowledge of hieroglyphs spread, so symbols were identified in cartouches on the walls of the tombs and the names of their owners were revealed. Finally the world was introduced to Pharaoh Akhenaten who had lived in this remote, desert area with his wife Nefertiti and their daughters. His city was known as Akhetaten, the City of the Horizon. Akhenaten lived around 1350BC and we are told that, after his death, his successors tried hard to erase all trace of him. There were few monuments left still bearing his name, and few records of his life, yet today he is equally as famous as Ramses and Cleopatra.

In this chapter we need to examine the history of the late 18th Dynasty. It is important to understand this history and to gain an insight into where Akhenaten came from. Akhenaten is one of the most fascinating people to emerge from Ancient Egypt, and more books have been written about him than any other Pharaoh. He is, at different times, considered to be a deformed figure with elongated limbs; he is really a woman; he destroyed his country by refusing to defend its borders; he changed the religion of his people; he was really Moses or Joseph from the bible. Any combination of

Chapter 1

these descriptions can be heard whenever Akhenaten's name is mentioned, but no-one seems able to give a decisive biography of this intriguing figure.

Most Egyptologists accept that Akhenaten was the son of Amenhotep III and his chief wife Tiy. We know quite a lot about Amenhotep III and his place in history as he is well documented in the chronology of the 18th Dynasty. However, this documentation does not reveal much about his family life. The Eighteenth Dynasty (approx 1550-1300 BC) is perhaps the best known of all the dynasties of ancient Egypt, and includes Tutankhamen who became famous when his tomb was discovered by Howard Carter in 1922.

This Dynasty was founded by **Ahmose** and during his reign Egypt was finally liberated from the rule of the hated Hyksos who had moved into Egypt and gradually taken power. Ahmose's mummy has been discovered and was very well preserved. It suggests he was about 35 years old when he died.

Ahmose was given the birth name, or **nomen** Ah-mose (The Moon is Born).

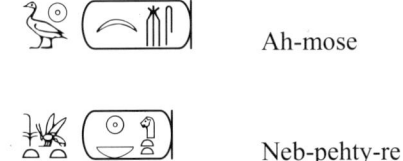

Ah-mose

Neb-pehty-re

His throne name or **prenomen** was Neb-pehty-re (The Lord of Strength is Re) and he was probably only a boy when he assumed the thrown, having lost his father Seqenenre Taa II, the last king of the 17th dynasty, and his brother Kahmose within three years of each other. So he was probably only about 10 years old when he succeeded his father.

His mother was Queen Ashotep, a powerful woman who was his co-

Amarna --- the missing evidence

regent during his early years. It was not uncommon for Pharaoh's mother to be co-regent if he came to the throne whilst still a child.

Egyptologists believe that during his very early reign, little was probably accomplished, and that in the ongoing battle with the Hyksos, they may have even gained some ground and recaptured Heliopolis. By the end of his tenth year in power, however, he laid siege on Avaris, the Hyksos' capital city. Ahmose, son of Ibana, a naval officer from El-Kab, wrote about the battle on the walls of his tomb at El Kab.

This was a long battle, and Ahmose was often fighting on several fronts at the same time. He had to put down insurrections in already liberated territories, but he was finally successful sometime between his 12th and 15th year as ruler. Ahmose was a warrior like his father and brother, and the siege was not the end of his adventures. He went on to attack the southwest Palestinian fortress of Sharuhen, entering a six year siege that would finally put an end to Hyksos control of Egypt.

After this, he attacked Nubia in the south and, while his brother may have gained some ground before he died, Ahmose pushed south to the Second Cataract. Here, he established a new centre at Buhen. This was ruled by a Viceroy named Djehuty. While Ahmose was in Nubia, former Hyksos allies again attempted a few uprising in the north, but this was soon put down. Ahmose's mother, Ashotep, was probably responsible for organising this and she was awarded the "gold fly" for courage which was found with her mummy in her tomb at Thebes.

Ahmose married his sister, Ahmose-Nefertari. This was not uncommon, and such a marriage cemented his right to the throne. Ahmose-Nefertari was the Royal Heiress, the eldest daughter of Ahmose and Ashotep. The couple had several children including Amenhotep who was to become the second Pharaoh of the Eighteenth Dynasty. Ahmose's tomb has never been found in the Valley of the Kings, and a mortuary temple recently

Chapter 1

excavated at Abydos suggests that he was initially buried there. However his mummy was found in the Deir el-Bahri Cache in 1881. A linen docket found on the mummy wrappings of Ahmose tell us that he was "osirified" in Year 8 of Pharaoh Psusennes I of the 21st dynasty.

Ahmose's son **Amenhotep I** ascended to the throne at a relatively young age, for two elder brothers had died before their father. He served brief co-regency with his father, but his mother certainly played an important part in his reign, acting on his behalf while he was still a child.

Fig. 1.1 Pharaoh Amenhotep I with his mother queen Ahmose-Nefertari.

Unlike his father and grandfather, Amenhotep I had a fairly peaceful reign. He faced a Libyan uprising his first year as king, but he had no problem in dealing with it. We learn from inscriptions provided by Ahmose son of Ebana, backed up by Ahmose-Pen-Nekhbet, that Amenhotep I also led a military expedition into Nubia in about year eight of his reign. He went past

Amarna --- the missing evidence

the second cataract of the Nile, and brought captives back to Thebes. He appointed a man named Turi as Viceroy of Kush, and established a temple marking Egypt's southern boundary at the Nubian down of Sai. As much of his reign was so peaceful, Amenhotep I was able to devote a great amount of time to commissioning the building of temples along the Nile to the god Amun. Thebes was now the capital of Egypt and Amenhotep was responsible for commissioning the great temple at Karnak. It would seem that by the end of Amenhotep I's reign, the main characteristics of the 18th Dynasty had been established, including a clear devotion to the cult of Amun at Karnak. This clearly figured predominantly later on in the life of Akhenaten.

Fig 1.2 *Amenhotep I from the tomb of Ahmose Nefertari.*

His **nomen** Amenhotep means "Amun is satisfied"

Chapter 1

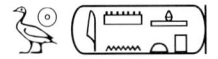

His throne name or **prenomen** was Djeser Ka re "Holy is the Soul of Re"

Evidence has been found that suggests Amenhotep I's son died in infancy, but it is possible that he had no children at-all. At any rate, his military commander, **Tuthmoses I** who was married to the king's sister, Princess Ahmose, came to the throne when Amenhotep I died. Tuthmoses was possibly a grandson of Ahmose, but he gained the right to the throne through this marriage to the Royal Heiress.

Tuthmoses means "Born of the god Thoth",

whilst his **prenomen** was A-Kheper-ka.-re, which means "Great is the Soul of Re."

Tuthmoses I was quite old when he became Pharaoh, and only ruled for about six years. Those six years were action packed, though, and his greatest campaigns were in the Delta. His battles were against the Syrians as he finally reached the Euphrates River, and this expedition opened new horizons that led later to Egypt's important role in the trade and diplomacy of the Late Bronze Age Near East. His wife, Ahmose bore him two sons named

Amarna --- the missing evidence

Wadjmose and Amenmose but they predeceased their father; so it was by Mutnofret a minor queen who was the sister of his principle wife, Ahmose, that his heir, Tuthmoses II was born. However, his more famous offspring was Queen Hatshepsut, a daughter by Ahmose who would rule after her husband and brother's death. Hatshepsut will be important to our understanding of events later in the Eighteenth Dynasty.

As the son of a minor wife, **Tuthmoses II** earned the right to the throne by marrying his half sister, The Royal Heiress Hatshepsut. We are now entering a period of Egyptian history that has as many stories woven round it as Akhenaten's reign has. Hatshepsut is portrayed as a proud, royal Heiress, fiercely loyal to her father and her ancestors. So devoted was she to her father that she supposedly chose to be buried with him.

Tuthmoses II is described by some authors as a sickly king constantly overshadowed by his queen, a future Pharaoh of Egypt, Hatshepsut. He did mount a military campaign against the Asiatics and entered Syria with the Egyptian army, though.

As we saw with his father, Tuthmoses' **nomen** means "born of the god Thoth",

whilst his **prenomen** follows the same theme A-Kheper-n-re. "Great is the form of Re."

Tuthmoses II and Hatshepsut produced a child, a girl, Neferure, but no sons. A boy, Tuthmoses, was born to a secondary wife, Isis, and when Tuthmoses II dies it is this boy who was crowned as Pharaoh aged 12.

Hatshepsut became the twelve year old Pharaoh **Tuthmoses III**'s

Chapter 1

co-regent and went on to rule Egypt alone. She married him to her daughter, Neferure, the Royal Heiress who could trace her bloodline directly back to Ahmose-Nefertari. This has given rise to many "wicked stepmother" theories, and we are told that because of this, later rulers did not include her name on their "Kings Lists". (2)

Of course the reason could have been because they did not recognise a female Pharaoh, but is more likely that is was because Tuthmoses III had been crowned as Pharaoh *before* Hatshepsut took control and declared herself to be the rightful Pharaoh. This move may have been welcomed by the people, as a child on the throne could not have been good for the country. She did not take the throne *before* her step-son, or rule *after* him. She had no place in the chronology.

Fig 1.3. Replica of the Abydos Kings' List at the British Museum.

Amarna --- the missing evidence

Tuthmoses III was yet another Tuthmoses, 🐦 (𓇳𓏺𓏺) this time with the throne name or **prenomen** of Men-Kheper-re "Lasting is the manifestation of Re."

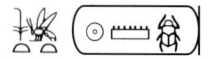

Whilst Tuthmoses III waited in the background, Hatshepsut proved herself a very capable ruler. She commissioned a great many buildings, including two obelisks to her father at Karnak and two more later to celebrate her sixteenth year as Pharaoh. Temples were built and restored, but the masterpiece of Hatshepsut's commissions was her mortuary temple complex at Deir el-Bahri. This still stands as tribute to her abilities. She was no shrinking violet and left records everywhere of her achievements – often exaggerated. Hatshepsut assumed all of the regalia and symbols of Pharaoh in official representations: the Khat head cloth, topped with the uraeus the traditional false beard, and shendyt kilt. Her name was sometimes written in the masculine and sometimes in the feminine depending on whether the writer actually knew her correct gender. This is worth noting as we will see it again in Chapter Eight.

Hatshepsut's **nomen** means "Foremost of Noble Ladies"

and she chose a different style of **prenomen** Maat-Ka-re "Truth is the Soul of Re."

Chapter 1

Fig 1.4. *Tuthmoses III at the Cairo Museum.*

Fig 1.5. *Hatshepsut*

Amarna --- the missing evidence

Once she became Pharaoh herself, Hatshepsut proclaimed that she was her father's designated successor with inscriptions on the walls of her mortuary temple:

Then his majesty said to them: "This daughter of mine, Khnumetamun Hatshepsut—may she live!—I have appointed as my successor upon my throne... she shall direct the people in every sphere of the palace; it is she indeed who shall lead you. Obey her words, unite yourselves at her command." The royal nobles, the dignitaries, and the leaders of the people heard this proclamation of the promotion of his daughter, the King of Upper and Lower Egypt, Maatkare—may she live eternally.

Hatshepsut ruled for approximately 22 years and during this time Tuthmoses III appears to have been quite content with his role as Head of the Army. He was clearly a military man who later became known as Egypt's Napoleon, owing to his military prowess and his height (or more correctly, his lack of height.) Tuthmoses III finally took control of the throne of Egypt as a man of about 34 years of age. It would appear from inscriptions that he was much loved by his people, respected as a great warrior, and was known as a sincere and fair minded leader. Tuthmoses III is known as one of the greatest of Egyptian rulers because he was able to re-established Egyptian control over Syria and Nubia. He went on to rule alone for another 30 years. We are told that he defaced Hatshepsut's cartouches and figures in an effort to erase her memory; but more on this later.

Amenhotep II was the son of Tuthmoses III and a minor wife, Merytre-Hatshepsut. He was not the oldest son of this Pharaoh though, but his elder brother Amenemhat, the son of the great king's chief wife Satiah, had died. Satiah herself died at about the same time which led some Egyptologists to consider this rather suspicious. Strange that mother and son

Chapter 1

should die at the same time. After becoming Pharaoh, Amenhotep married a woman of unknown parentage named Tiaa As many as ten sons and one daughter have been attributed to him, but his most important son was Tuthmoses IV, who succeeded him.

Amenhotep is a traditional family name,

and this Pharaoh chose the throne name or **prenomen** of A-Kheper-u-re "Great are the manifestations of Re.

A co regency with Tuthmoses III and Amenhotep II is believed to have lasted for two years and four months.

In his seventh year, Amenhotep was faced with a rebellion in Syria by the vassal states of Naharin and he sent his army to battle. This rebellion was started by Egypt's chief Near Eastern rival, Mitanni. After the battles in Amenhotep's ninth year, the Egyptian and Mitannian armies never fought again, and the two kingdoms lived on in mutual respect. This relationship is very important when we come to examine the end of the Amarna period. Amenhotep II was followed by yet another Tuthmoses.

The length of **Tuthmoses IV**'s reign is not entirely clear. It is thought that he ruled for 9 or 10 years, but it may be that he ruled for longer. Tuthmoses IV was born to Amenhotep II and Tiaa but was not actually the crown prince or Amenhotep II's chosen successor to the throne.

Amarna --- the missing evidence

Fig 1.6. Tuthmoses IV and his mother Tiaa. Cairo Museum

Tuthmoses may have ousted his older brother in order to usurp power and then commissioned the *Dream Stelae* in order to justify his unexpected kingship. The Dream Stelae tells the story of how, after a day's hunting, Tuthmoses fell asleep by the Sphinx at Giza. He dreamt that the Sphinx asked him to clear the sand that was covering him, and that if Tuthmoses did this, then the Sphinx would make him King.

Fig 1.7. *The Dream Stelae, Giza.*

Chapter 1

The text of the stelae reads:

Once upon a time he practised spear-throwing for pleasure in the territory of the Memphite, in its southern and northern limits, where he threw bolts at the target, and hunted lions in the valley of the gazelles. He rode in his two-horsed chariot, and his horses were faster than the wind. With him were two of his attendants. No-one knew who they were.

Then came the time when he allowed his servants to rest. He took advantage of this to present to Horemkhu, near the temple of Seker in the city of the dead, and to the goddess Rannu, an offering of the flower and to pray to the great mother Isis, the lady of the north wall and the lady of the south wall, and to Sekhet of Xois, and to Set. For a great enchantment lay in this place from the beginning of time, as far as the districts of the lords of Babylon, the sacred road of the gods to the western horizon of On-Heliopolis, because the form of the Sphinx is a likeness of Kheper-Ra, the very great god who lives in this place, the greatest of all spirits, the most venerable being who rests upon it. To him the residents of Memphis and all of the towns in his district raise their hands to pray before his countenance, and to offer him important sacrifices.

On one of these days it happened, when the king's son Tuthmoses had arrived on his journey about mid-day, and had stretched himself to rest in the shade of this great god, that sleep overtook him. He dreamt in his slumber at the moment when the sun was at the zenith, and it seemed to him as though this great god spoke to him with his own mouth, just as a father speaks to his son, addressing him thus:-
' Behold me, look at me, thou, my son Tuthmoses. I am your father Horemkhu, Kheper, Ra, Tmu. The kingdom shall be given to you, and you shall wear the white crown and the red crown on the throne of the earth-god Seb, the youngest among the gods. The world shall be yours in its length and

Amarna --- the missing evidence

in its breadth, as far as the light of the eye of the lord of the universe shines. Plenty and riches shall be yours; the best from the interior of the land, and rich tributes from all nations; long years shall be granted to you as your term of life. My countenance is gracious towards you, and my heart clings to you; I will give you the best of all things.

'The sand of the area in which I live has covered me up. Promise me that you will do what I wish in my heart; then shall I know whether you are my son, my helper. Go forward let me be united with you.

After this Tuthmoses awoke, and he repeated all these speeches, and he understood the meaning of the words of the god and laid them up in his heart, speaking thus with himself: 'I see how the inhabitants in the temple of the city honour this god with important gifts, without thinking of freeing from sand the work of King Khaf-Ra, the statue which was made to Tmu-Horemkhu.

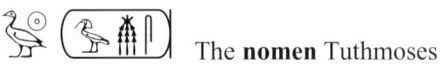

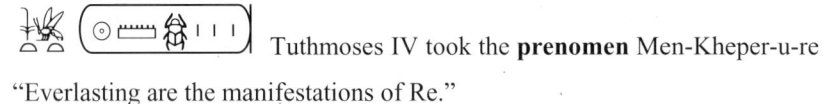

The **nomen** Tuthmoses

Tuthmoses IV took the **prenomen** Men-Kheper-u-re "Everlasting are the manifestations of Re."

Tuthmoses IV was buried in the Valley of the Kings, in tomb KV43, but his body was later moved to the mummy cache in Amenhotep II's tomb, KV35, where it was discovered by Victor Loret in 1898. An examination of his body shows that he was very ill and had been wasting away for the final months of his life prior to his death, probably suffering from a form of cancer.

Amenhotep III came to the throne of Egypt as a child, sometime between the ages of two and twelve years of age. There is a statue of the treasurer Sobekhotep holding a prince Amenhotep-mer-khepseh that was

Chapter 1

made shortly before Tuthmoses IV's death, as well as a painting in the tomb of the royal nurse, Hekarnehhe (TT64) which shows the prince as a young boy. This suggests that he was probably aged between six and twelve years of age at the time of his father's death. So, as the son of Tuthmoses IV and his minor wife Mutemwia, Amenhotep III became king with his mother acting as regent.

The third Amenhotep chose the **prenomen** Neb-Maat-Re "Lord of truth is Re."

You may have noticed that when speaking of the buildings attributed to the Pharaohs, I have used the word "commissioned" not "built" by them. We are told that Amenhotep III "built" extensively at Luxor and Karnak, dedicating temples to the god Amun. This has caused a lot of confusion over where he spent his life and where he raised his family. Amenhotep III did not build these wonderful temples. He is unlikely to have ever picked up a chisel to carve out his messages! These buildings were "commissioned." In the same way, in 1508 Pope Julius II commissioned the painting of the ceiling of the Sistine Chapel by Michelangelo, but the builders of the temples were unknown.

We do not know where Amenhotep III grew up, but it was more likely to have been in Memphis than Thebes. His father, Tuthmoses IV seems to have preferred Memphis to Thebes and Amenhotep III took the throne as a child. A few records survive from Amenhotep IIIs early years as Pharaoh, but give no indication as to where he was living. Quarry inscriptions survive

Amarna --- the missing evidence

from years 1 and 2, and a tax document from year 5. In year 10 two commemorative bulletins were issued to announce the arrival of Gilukhipa, the daughter of Shutarna, King of Naharin, and in year 11 we learn of the making of a lake for his wife, Queen Tiy.

Fig 1.8. A very young Amenhotep III with his mother, Mutemwia.

Chapter 1

An inscription proclaiming the appointment of Neb- Nefer as "chief measurer of the granary of god's offering of Amun" tells us that in his year 20, Amenhotep was in Memphis. Around year 30 things changed. Amenhotep III celebrated his first jubilee. Over 200 jar labels mentioning this celebration have been found at the Malkata palace, which would strongly suggest that he was living in Thebes at the time. Very little is known of Amenhotep III before year 30, but after that date there is a continuous flow.

There have been no datable records found to show that Amenhotep III spent any amount of time in Thebes early in his reign. The Priests of Amun were very much in charge and gaining power. For Amenhotep III to move there from Memphis must arouse some curiosity. If he was so attached to Memphis, why move? When he did move, he did not move to the centre of Thebes. He did not move to the palaces of his ancestors. His new palace was built at Malkata – away from the established, traditional royal residences. This was a place which had never been used before – a virgin site which had not been used in histories times. Why? Had the plague started to take hold?

When going on to study the lives of Akhenaten, Nefertiti and their family, this knowledge is important. It shows that Akhenaten most probably spent his childhood and youth at Memphis and influenced by the sun cult of Re at Heliopolis. His father moved to ***"a virgin site which had not been used in historic times."*** which is **exactly** what Akhenaten did a little later.

Unless the authorities give permission to dig up modern day Cairo, we are unlikely to know much more. However, who knows in the future if technology might enable us to discover the many treasures under those busy streets.

This is only a brief introduction to the Pharaohs of the eighteenth dynasty, but it does have a purpose. It shows that with few exceptions, every Pharaoh formed part of a co-regency – either with their father, their mother or

Amarna --- the missing evidence

their wife. Hatshepsut was Tuthmoses IIIs step-mother, but the principle still holds. It also makes us wonder about infant mortality at the time. These Pharaohs lived to a good age yet so many were succeeded by a child. It is unlikely that they practiced celibacy until their thirties, or that there was a wonderful form of birth control: so what happened to the older children? One theory has to be that they died from disease. Diseases such as Influenza appear in Egypt in the 18th Dynasty, and plague was rife. Yet as we move into the reign of Amenhotep IV, Egyptologists dismiss the idea of a co-regency as absurd.

Let us now examine the popular story of Amenhotep IV. Better known as Akhenaten, Amenhotep IV was the most unusual Pharaoh to ever rule Egypt. He led the county in a direction that would make later generations tag him "the Rebel". Akhenaten introduced new ideas in religion and art that would leave a lasting impression on the world. Unlike most Pharaohs, Akhenaten presented himself in a way that would lead to controversy, and would shock the establishment. Instead of a calm, handsome Pharaoh, Akhenaten was portrayed as a pot bellied, elongated figure with breasts and an egg shaped head.

Akhenaten's wife was Nefertiti. The Couple had six daughters named Merytaten, Ankhesenpaaten, Meketaten, Neferneferuaten-tasharit, Neferneferure, and Setepenre. As a young child Akhenaten was raised in a traditional Ancient Egyptian manner and observed religious rituals to the god Amun. In Thebes, Amun was the god who was elevated to the highest position. In time, though, Akhenaten turned his focus and beliefs to another deity called the Aten.

Yet another Amenhotep, his throne name Nefer-Kheper-u-re also followed in the family tradition, meaning "Beautiful are the manifestations of Re." The Aten, the sun-disk, first appears in texts dating to the 12th dynasty in The Story of Sinuhe where the deceased king is described as rising as god

Chapter 1

to the heavens and uniting *with the sun-disk, the divine body merging with its maker.*

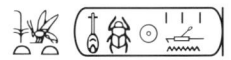

This Pharaoh later changed his **nomen** to Akhenaten which means "Servant of the Aten."

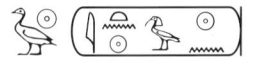

Fig 1.9. *Statue of Amenhotep IV/Akhenaten.*

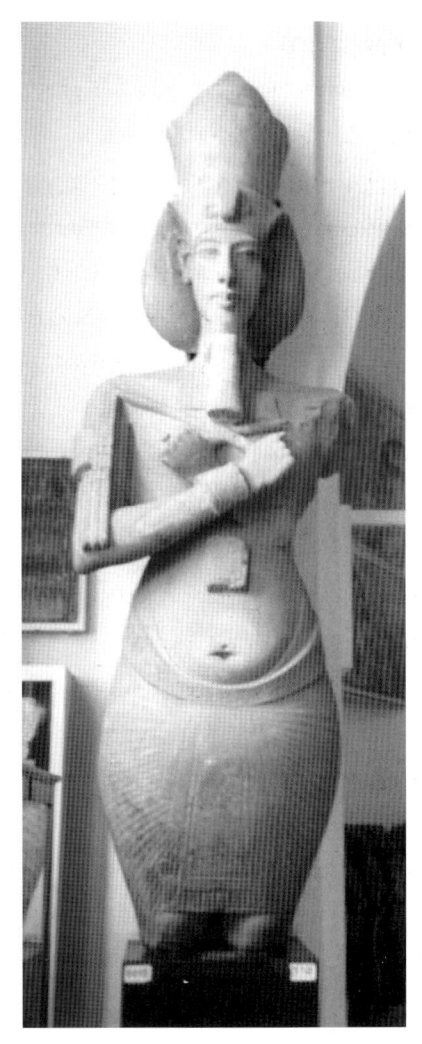

Amarna --- the missing evidence

Soon after becoming Pharaoh of Egypt, Akhenaten discarded his royal name and loyalty to Amun. He turned away from old priests and began the cult of the sun disk - the Aten. Akhenaten believed that Aten was the only god, and he claimed he was the only person able to speak to his god. There was no need for priests, and he soon banished those that looked after the temples at Luxor and Thebes. He banned the worship of Amun and closed down sacred temples. Akhenaten's wife's name Nefertiti was also changed to "Nefer Neferu Aten" meaning "Beautiful is the Beauty of Aten." The couple then moved out of Thebes to a new capital called Akhetaten. Everyone from the old capital moved to the new constructed capital including the court and artisans.

Akhenaten's new city Akhetaten was built in honour of the god Aten. (Amarna is the modern name for the site of the city called Akhetaten) Art in the new city portrayed natural scenes and life-like figures. The couple commissioned the building of many palaces and temples, and held ceremonies in them. Akhenaten attacked the cults of other deities in Egypt, especially Amun. Sites of Amun were desecrated and any evidence of worship to this god destroyed.

Akhenaten even had his father's cartouches destroyed because they had Amun's name pictured on them. This behaviour continued to outrage the people of Egypt and left the people uneasy and angry. Most of the cities in Egypt were deprived of their estates and plantations. Corruption was rife in the temples and soon everyone was dependant on the city of Akhetaten.

The art during the Amarna period had made a colossal change. People were portrayed as they really were. Unlike most Pharaohs, Akhenaten portrayed himself less like a god and more like a human. This new style of art portrayed the Royal Family involved in everyday activities and women featured prominently.

Bek was Akhenaten's main artist during this period. The disfigured

Chapter 1

Pharaoh showed a strange elongation of the head, large breasts and a swollen stomach He looked more like a woman than a man. Many early explorers believed that this Pharaoh **was** a woman.

Not only did Akhenaten show his "back to nature" image, but as mentioned above, the paintings and carvings at Akhetaten show more natural images. His paintings were detailed and unique in that they showed nature along the Nile River. The scenes showed the river and the land covered with vegetation and wild animals, yet the city of Akhetaten was built on desert sand.

Fig 1.10. *Fragment showing the Royal Couple with three of their children.*
(more about this later)

Amarna --- the missing evidence

Pharaohs from earlier periods showed themselves as being well proportioned and taller then their subjects. Akhenaten, on the other hand, was shown as a strange figure, and portrayed him in scenes never before imagined. Such scenes included him kissing his daughters and sitting with his wife and family eating meals.

During the 12th year of his reign, his mother, Queen Tiy, joined Akhenaten in his city. She brought with her a princess named Beketaten (Later Beketamun). Akhenaten built a temple in her honour, and as Nefertiti was no longer Akhenaten's chief wife, she soon disappeared from the scene. Historians are puzzled as to why and where she left. Her oldest daughter, Merytaten, soon took her place and held the duties her mother once did. This daughter was then replaced with his second daughter, Ankhesenpaaten. Akhenaten found anther queen who was named Kiya and might have been the daughter of Tushratta of Mitanni. Kiya became the mother of Tutankhamen. In about the eighteenth year of his reign Akhenaten died. Everything was destroyed and demolished by his enemies soon after his death. His mummy has never been found.

But is that really so? Does this really make sense? Read on and decide for yourself.

Chapter 1

Notes:

1.The Rosetta Stone was discovered in 1799 by French scholars brought into Egypt by Napoleon. The soldiers were demolishing an ancient wall in the town of Rosetta to clear the way for an extension to the fort, but built into the wall was a stone bearing a remarkable set of inscriptions. The same piece of writing had been inscribed on the stone in three different languages – Greek, Demotic and Hieroglyphs. Scholars could read Greek and the translation soon revealed that the Rosetta Stone contained a decree from the general council of Egyptian priests issued in 196 BC. An Englishman, Thomas Young took up the challenge of deciphering the hieroglyphs in 1814, and he was able to match up the letters of "Ptolemy" with the hieroglyphs. Young's work was not progressing fast enough and the challenge was picked up by Jean-François Champollion who used Young's techniques to finally decipher the hieroglyphs in 1822.

2.Kings Lists. The Abydos Kings list gives the 18th dynasty Kings as:

Neb-pehty-re (Ahmose)   Djeserkare (Amenhotep I)

Aa-Kheper-kare (Tuthmoses I)   Aa-Kheper-en-re (Tuthmoses II)

Menkheperre (Tuthmoses III)   Aa-kheperu-re (Amenhotep II)

Men-kheperure (Tuthmoses IV)   Neb-maat-re (Amenhotep III)

Djeser-kheperu-re Setep-en-er (Horemheb)

Chapter 2

The Founding of Akhetaten

"We require from buildings, as from men, two kinds of goodness: first, the doing their practical duty well: then that they be graceful and pleasing in doing it; which last is itself another form of duty." --- **John Ruskin.**

The City of the Aten. The "Horizon of the Aten." The city on the site of modern day El Amarna was the creation of a Pharaoh of Ancient Egypt, Amenhotep IV. A new city, built in the blazing dessert, hundreds of miles from the established capital and the established gods. A city where he could live with his wife and family, enjoying the fruits of life and worshipping his favourite god.

But Pharaohs just don't do things like that, do they? Pharaohs are there to bridge the gap between the common people and the Gods. They are there to ensure that the gods are pleased and thus ensure good harvests with food for the people. Their role is to ensure the country is safe from invaders – and even to conquer a few neighbouring states if the time is right. Pharaohs are not meant to select new Gods, or to uproot capital cities at a whim and move from an established, fertile area to the blazing heat of the Egyptian desert. Nevertheless, the new city was built.

Let us start here by trying to understand what really happened at the start of the reign of Amenhotep IV.

We know from excavations at Karnak that the young Amenhotep IV began his reign living in Thebes and commissioning the building of temples as his father Amenhotep III had done. Life for our young Pharaoh must have been comfortable, as Egypt was a very prosperous country. Earlier Pharaohs

Amarna --- the missing evidence

of the 18th dynasty had fought wars to keep out foreigners or to win territory, and consequently few, if any military actions were called for during his father's reign. Amenhotep III appears to have spent his early life as a sportsman, and his later life as a foreign diplomat. Much of Egypt's wealth came from foreign trade, and so life, certainly for royalty and the nobility, must have been very pleasant. Little is known of the lives of the ordinary people, but Amenhotep III was remembered hundreds of years later, as a fertility god, who was worshipped to bring about agricultural success. It would seem likely that harvests during his reign were good. The Gods were pleased.

Temples at Karnak and Luxor were dedicated to the god Amun. During the Twelfth dynasty, Amun was adopted in Thebes with Mut as his consort. Amun and Mut had one child, the moon god Khonsu. Amun was promoted to national god by Ahmose, the founder of the 18th Dynasty; because the king believed that he had helped him drive the Hyksos from Egypt.

We are often told that Amenhotep IV changed his name to Akhenaten and founded a new religion, worshipping the god Aten. The ancient Egyptian term for the disk of the sun was "Aten," which is first seen during the Middle Kingdom (although solar worship begins much earlier in Egyptian history.) So whilst his change of name is correct, it is not true that Akhenaten founded the new religion. Quite clearly, his father, Amenhotep III and his Grandfather Tuthmoses IV were involved in the worship of the Aten. Even his Great-Grandfather, Amenhotep II showed a real interest in this god. Amenhotep III was determined that he be identified with this sun god during his lifetime and he even named his palace "the gleaming Aten." Amenhotep commissioned great improvements at Karnak as part of his nationwide building programme, but the sun was also worshipped as the solar disc the Aten. The king showed his love of this god by taking the epithet

Chapter 2

'Dazzling Aten'. But this did seem to be kept as a personal preference. Amenhotep III continued to commission the building of temples and dedicate them to the god Amun. The priests of Amun might not have liked Akhenaten's actions too much, and probably said so; but the status quo was maintained. This desire to be identified with the sun probably came from the time Amenhotep III spent living in Memphis.

The reign of the Pharaoh Amenhotep III marked the high point of ancient Egyptian civilisation, both in terms of political power and cultural achievement. Early in his reign Amenhotep III was married to Tiy, the daughter of a provincial official named Yuya and his wife Tuya, and for the rest of the reign Queen Tiy featured prominently alongside the king. The marriage was announced on what has become known as the "Marriage Scarab". Some say this was a love match, but Amenhotep and Tiy were still very young children and it is far more likely that his mother, Mutemwia, selected Tiy from among the suitable, available young ladies of the Court. A relationship with the royal family of Mitanni seems very likely, as Mutemwia was most probably the daughter of King Artatama of Mitanni.

Fig 2.1 The marriage scarab.

Amarna --- the missing evidence

The marriage scarab tells us:

Long live King Amenhotep, who is given life, and the Great King's Wife Tiy, who lives... The name of her father is Yuya, the name of her mother is Tuya. She is the wife of a mighty king, whose southern boundary is as far as Karoy, and his northern as far as Mitanni.

Tiy could have been related to the Royal Family in some way, as one of the most intriguing questions in Egyptian history remains unanswered. **What happened to brothers and sisters of Pharaoh?** In modern society, the brothers and sisters of kings marry and have their own families. Yet we hear nothing of these siblings of Pharaohs. As Amenhotep III commissioned the improvement and development of Karnak as part of his nationwide building programme, so Amun's clergy became more and more powerful. Pharaoh could not have been happy with this: no-one should be more powerful than Pharaoh! Amenhotep III turned to the sun disc, the Aten.

Back then to our young Pharaoh Amenhotep IV. What do we know of his early life? The answer is, very little. There is no recorded evidence of him as a child, and he has never been shown with his parents. As we have suggested, much could still be discovered under the streets of Cairo. Amenhotep IV never claims to be the son of Amenhotep III at all, although in many of his inscriptions he does speak fondly of his mother, Queen Tiy, who was Amenhotep III's, chief wife. We know that Amenhotep IV had sisters, Sitamun, Henuttaneb, Isis or Iset and Nebetah, as these are shown on statues with his parents.

We are told that he had an older brother, Tuthmoses, but there is no clear evidence that this is true. He is mentioned in a papyrus now at the British Museum, but this is perhaps our first clear example of something being taken out of context and turned into part of the history of Akhenaten. He is named as: *Crown Prince Tuthmoses, ,Eldest King's Son,*

Chapter 2

High Priest of Ptah at Memphis, Sem-Priest of Ptah at Memphis, and Overseer of the Prophets of Upper and Lower Egypt.

Fig 2.2. Prince Tuthmoses on his bier.

There is absolutely no evidence anywhere that this Tuthmoses was the son of Amenhotep III or older brother of Akhenaten. Akhenaten could have been the only son of the family, or he could have had a younger brother, which I explore further in Chapter 10.

Amenhotep IV definitely started his reign at Thebes. One of his first commissioned building projects was the Gem-pa-Aten. It was constructed outside the boundaries of the temples of Amun-Re to the east.

Amarna --- the missing evidence

Fig 2.3. This colossal statue shows Amenhotep III, Queen Tiy and thereof their daughters.

Chapter 2

The name **Gem-pa-aten** means "The Sun Disc is found in the Estate of the God Aten". Amenhotep IV might have moved to the Gem-pa-Aten when the building was completed, and during these early years, he was engaged in commissioning several other building projects. These included temples to the Aten in other parts of Egypt, particularly at Memphis and at Sesebi in Nubia. One of the buildings within the Gem-pa-Aten complex .is the Hut-benben ('Mansion of the Benben') which seems to have been a temple devoted to his wife, Nefertiti. The couple's eldest daughter Merytaten appears with her mother on these temple walls.

So what happened to change all this? So far, we have seen a young Pharaoh, living a life of luxury, married, with two daughters, and happily building temples, to his God. What a life! What privilege. Something others could only dream of. Yet he was not happy. Eventually he left this idyllic existence and moved north to create a new city in the desert. Why? What prompted such drastic action? And to what use was the new city to be put?

Why was the site in the desert chosen? Akhenaten tells us that it was the Aten that chose the site. The Aten had directed him there. One idea has been suggested that on approaching Akhetaten from the Nile there is a gap in the cliffs which looks like the hieroglyph for "Horizon."
This may be so, but it does not seem very likely.
More likely was his urge to find *"a place which had not been used in historic times"* as his father had done before him. Was plague one reason for his move? A virgin site – uncontaminated by disease?

Four years at Thebes, then something certainly happened. A desire to avoid the plague would have been one very good reason for a move, but there was probably also a problem with the priesthood of Amun at Thebes. Did they object to the new temples dedicated to the Aten being built within a temple complex dedicated to the ancient God Amun? The priests were

Amarna --- the missing evidence

certainly very powerful and would have been ruthless in their determination to maintain that power.

Amenhotep IV changed his name to Akhenaten and began work on his new City. Having decided on a desert region, hundreds of miles from Thebes, he marked out the site by building "Boundary stelae". The boundary stelae took the form of rock inscriptions in the cliffs around Akhetaten 'the horizon of the Aten'.

We do not know for sure how many boundary stelae were erected, but we do know that the surviving stelae were built at different times. The early stelae were built in year 5, and all have the "early" proclamation carved into the surface of the rock. . In this early proclamation Akhenaten tells of certain unpleasantness back in Thebes.

He had heard "words" and these words were:
It was worse than those of which I heard in regnal year 4
It was worse than those which I heard in regnal, year 3
It was worse than those which I heard in regnal year 2
It was worse than those which are in there, Neb-maat-re heard
It was worse than those which are in there, Ahkheprure heard
It was worse than those which are in there, Menkhepererre heard and
It was worse than those heard by any king who had ever assumed the White Crown

Neb-maat-re was his father Amenhotep III. Menkheperure was his grandfather, Thutmose IV Ahkheperure was his great-grandfather Amenhotep II What had these Pharaohs in common that was so dreadful? It was during the reign of Amenhotep II that the earliest image of Aten appears on a monument at Giza as a winged sun disk with outstretched arms holding the cartouche of the Pharaoh. As we saw in chapter 1, Tuthmoses IV built his "Dream stelae" at Giza and this shows the winged sun disk. (fig. 1.7 chapter 1) Amenhotep III was determined to have his name linked with this

Chapter 2

Aten during his lifetime, but he did not neglect the other gods, or tried to promote the Aten as the "sole God." It does seem, however, that the rise in popularity of the Aten displeased the powerful priests of Amun.

Fig. 24 The site of the city of Akhetaten today.
A barren, desert site.

The boundary stelae that Akhenaten built to mark out the site of his new city give us a lot of first hand evidence about Akhenaten, and how he was feeling at the time. He stated quite clearly on the stelae that he intended to spend the rest of his life in this new city, and that if by any chance he died out side of it, his body was to be returned to there for burial. You can see this later in the chapter. This is the place where he intended to settle and raise his family in peace and with his new god the Aten. At first reading, the stelae do

Amarna --- the missing evidence

not say that Akhenaten himself intended never to leave Akhetaten, rather that Akhetaten should remain the size it was when built. This proclamation was carved before the city was completed, though, so it could mean that if he died outside the city **before it was finished** then he must be brought back for burial. There is no record of Akhenaten ever leaving his new city until he returns to Thebes for his father's burial.

Sixteen boundary stelae are known at the moment, as a new discovery, boundary stelae H was made in 2006. Three of the boundary stelae are on the western side of the Nile and the rest are on the eastern side. They provide a wealth of information about Akhenaten and his feelings as he set out to build his new city. Two different "proclamations" are made on the stelae. The first or "early" proclamation is dated regnal year 5, 4th month of winter, day 13. Part of it reads:

On this day, when One was in Akhetaten, His Majesty appeared on the great chariot of electrum, setting off on a good road toward Akhetaten, his place of creation, which he made for himself that he might set within it every day. There was presented a great offering to the Father, the Aten, consisting of bread, beer, long and short horned cattle, calves, fowl, wine, fruits, incense, all kinds of fresh green plants, and everything good, in front of the mountain of Akhetaten.

The king addresses his gathered courtiers:

As the Aten is beheld, the Aten desires that there be made for him as a monument with an eternal and everlasting name. Now, it is the Aten, my father, who advised me concerning it, namely Akhetaten. No official has ever advised me concerning it, not any of the people who are in the entire land has ever advised me concerning it, to suggest making Akhetaten in this distant place. It was the Aten, my father, who advised me concerning it, so that it might be made for Him as Akhetaten. Behold, it is Pharaoh who has discovered it: not being the property of a god, not being the property of a

Chapter 2

goddess, not being the property of a ruler, not being the property of a female ruler, not being the property of any people to lay claim to it.   I shall make Akhetaten for the Aten, my father, in this place. I shall not make Akhetaten for him to the south of it, to the north of it, to the west of it, to the east of it. I shall not expand beyond the southern stelae of Akhetaten toward the south, nor shall I expand beyond the northern stelae of Akhetaten toward the north, in order to make Akhetaten for him there. Nor shall I make it for him on the western side of Akhetaten, but I shall make Akhetaten for the Aten, my father, on the east of Akhetaten, the place which He Himself made to be enclosed for Him by the mountain. I shall make the "House of the Aten" for the Aten, my father, in Akhetaten in this place. I shall make the "Mansion of the Aten" for the Aten, my father, in Akhetaten in this place. I shall make the Sun Temple of the Great King's Wife Neferneferuaten Nefertiti] for the Aten, my father, in Akhetaten in this place. I shall make the "House of Rejoicing" for the Aten, my father, in the "Island of the Aten, Distinguished in Jubilees" in Akhetaten in this place. I shall make for myself the apartments of Pharaoh., I shall make the apartments of the Great King's Wife in Akhetaten in this place.

Let a tomb be made for me in the eastern mountain of Akhetaten. Let my burial be made in it, in the millions of jubilees which the Aten, my father, has decreed for me. Let the burial of the Great King's Wife, Nefertiti, be made in it, in the millions of years which the Aten, my father, decreed for her. Let the burial of] the King's Daughter, Merytaten, be made in it, in these millions of years. If I die in any town downstream, to the south, to the west, to the east in these millions of years, let me be brought back, that I may be buried in Akhetaten. If the Great King's Wife, Nefertiti, dies in any town downstream, to the south, to the west, to the east in these millions of years, let her be brought back, that she may be buried in Akhetaten. If the King's Daughter, Merytaten, dies in any town downstream, to the south, to the west,

Amarna --- the missing evidence

to the east in the millions of years, let her be brought back, that she may be buried in Akhetaten. Let a cemetery for the Mnevis Bull be made in the eastern mountain of Akhetaten, that he may be buried in it. Let the tombs of the Chief of Seers, of the God's Fathers of the Aten be made in the eastern mountain of Akhetaten, that they may be buried in it. Let[the tombs of the priests of the Aten be made in the eastern mountain of Akhetaten that they may be buried in it'.

Both Boundary Stelae U shown below, and A shown on the next page, have Akhenaten's second proclamation engraved. This was mainly concerned with fixing even more securely the limits of Akhetaten and with dedicating all the enclosed land to the Aten.

This second proclamation is dated year 6, and it is this one that tells us what Akhenaten had planned for his City. This was clearly to be a city created by and dedicated to the Aten. The Aten gave Akhenaten instructions about how it was to be used.

Fig 2.5. Boundary Stelae U

Chapter 2

Fig 2.6 Boundary Stelae A.

Boundary Stelae A is found on the west bank of the Nile, and was the most northerly stelae to be built there. It is now protected by a glass cover, and clearly shows Akhenaten, Nefertiti, Merytaten and Ankhesenpaaten worshiping the Aten and dedicating an offering.

The Later (second) Proclamation.
On this day One was in Akhetaten in the mat tent made by his presence may he live, prosper and be well, in Akhetaten, called the Sun-disk is Content. Sunrise by his presence, may he live, prosper and be well, on horse, on the great chariot of fine gold the horizon,and has filled the two lands with his love. Moving ahead perfectly to Akhetaten, on the first time of discovering it

Amarna --- the missing evidence

by his presence, may he live, prosper and be well, for its foundation, as a monument to the sun disk as commanded by his father, the living Ra-Horakhty rejoicing in what is right ,in his name as Shu which is in the sun-disk, given life for ever and eternity, to make a monument for him within it. Causing there to be offered a great offering of bread and beer, oxen, cattle, bulls, birds, wine, fruit, incense, all good plants, on the day of foundation of Akhetaten for the living, like the sun disk when he rises from sun disk, who receives favours, who is loved for the life, prosperity and health of the dual king, who lives on what is right, lord of the two lands, Neferkheperure sole one of Ra, son of Ra, who lives on what is right, lord of sun-risings, Akhenaten, great in his lifespan, given life for ever and eternity. Proceeding south, resting by his presence, may he live, prosper, be well, on his chariot before his father the living Ra-Horakhty rejoicing in what is right, in his name as Shu which is in the sun-disk, given life for ever and eternity, on the south-eastern mountain of Akhetaten, with the rays of his father on him in life and power, making his body young every day.

The Oath

Oath spoken by the dual king, who lives on what is right, lord of the two lands, Neferkheperure sole one of Ra, son of Ra, who lives on what is right, lord of sun-risings, Akhenaten, great in his lifespan, given life for ever and eternity. As my father lives the living Ra-Horakhty rejoicing in what is right, in his name as Shu which is in the sun-disk, given life for ever and eternity, as my heart is sweetened over the king's wife, over her children, that old age be granted to the great king's wife Neferneferuaten Nefertiti granted life eternally, in this million years, while she is under the hand of Pharaoh may he live, prosper and be well, and old age be granted to the king's daughter Merytaten and the king's daughter Meketaten her children, while they are under the hand of the king's wife their mother for ever and eternity, my oath in truth, that I wish to say, that I do not say falsely, for ever

Chapter 2

and eternity: I will not break this oath that I have made for the sun-disk my father, for ever and eternity. It is now established on a stelae of stone on the south-eastern boundary, likewise on the north-eastern boundary of Akhetaten, and established likewise on a stelae of stone on the south-western boundary, likewise on the western boundary of Akhetaten. It is not to be hacked out, it is not to be washed away, it is not to be defaced, it is not to be plastered over; it is not to be made to vanish. If it fades, if it crumbles, if the stelae bearing it falls down, I will restore it back again in this place where it is.

So desperate is Akhenaten to move from Thebes, that he actually camps out on the site, whilst the city is being built. The later proclamation says: One was in Akhetaten in the **mat tent** This seems to be a very drastic action, and it would seem far more sensible to remain living in Thebes, whilst the new city is being built, but that is not the way it was done. Difficult to run a country from a tent.

Not satisfied with uprooting himself and his family, the young Amenhotep IV now changes his name to Akhenaten, meaning "Effective Spirit of the Aten" If the priests of Amun were upset before, they must be furious now! Their King – their Pharaoh! - abandoning the God Amun AND the temples of Karnak and Luxor (which provided them with great wealth) and disappearing hundreds of miles away to a barren desert site and a new God. So, a new city and a new life. Does he take trusted advisors with him? The men who have been the "Civil Service" of Egypt for years? That might help, as they would have influence at least. But no: most of the new Court is to be made up of previously unknown men, promoted to become the new Nobles. (See chapter 3)

So, we have a situation then where our Pharaoh Amenhotep IV uproots himself and his family, changes his **nomen** to Akhenaten, and camps out in the desert regions, whilst the new city is being built. The "Nobles" he

Amarna --- the missing evidence

takes with him are unknown and untested. Something was clearly going on. It may be wrong to say that Akhenaten "ran away" to Akhetaten, but it was clearly intended as a safe haven - **"a place which had not been used in historic times."**

In books about the 18th dynasty we are told that Akhenaten built his new city called Akhetaten soon after he took the throne after his father's death. He then moved to the capital city of Egypt from Thebes to this new city, and changed the religion of the country. Overnight, the people of Egypt were told to stop worshipping Amun or any of the old gods, and to start worshipping just one God, the Aten. No more Osiris, so no-one to oversee the "weighing of the heart" ceremony. The ancient Egyptians believed that when they died, they would be judged on their behaviour during their lifetime before they could be granted a place in the Afterlife. This judgement ceremony was called "Weighing of the Heart" and was recorded in Chapter 125 of the funerary text known as the "Book of the Dead".

The ceremony was believed to have taken place before Osiris, the chief god of the dead and Afterlife, and a jury of 43 gods. Standing before the tribunal the deceased was asked to name each member of the divine jury and swear that he or she had not committed any offence, ranging from shouting to stealing. This was the "negative confession". If found innocent, the deceased was declared "true of voice" and allowed to proceed into the Afterlife. The proceedings were recorded by Thoth, the scribe of the gods, and the god of wisdom. Thoth was often depicted as a human with an ibis head, writing on a scroll of papyrus. His other animal form, the baboon, was often shown sitting on the pivot of the scales of justice. But now there would be no more Anubis to carry out the weighing of the heart – so how could anyone secure everlasting life? In the Hall of Two Truths, the deceased's heart was weighed against the Shu feather of truth and justice taken from the headdress of the goddess Ma'at. If the heart was lighter than the feather, they could pass on,

Chapter 2

but if it were heavier they would be devoured by the demon Ammit. According to the ancient Egyptians, this scene shows what happens after a person has died, So. Are we to believe that all this changed? Overnight the beliefs of the people were disregarded and they were told to abandon their old gods.

Fig 2.7 The Weighing of the Heart ceremony from the Book of the Dead.

Could these changes have happened this way?

England has had its own Akhenaten; a king, who was full of his own self importance, and decided to change the religion of his country, England. We know him as Henry VIII. Like Akhenaten, Henry VIII, inherited a stable country, and at the King's finances were very health. He appeared to have everything: wealth, power and a beautiful wife, but like Akhenaten he was dissatisfied. Henry VIII, changed the religion of the country --- **and plunged it into turmoil!** People feared for their future. What would happen to them after death? Just as in Ancient Egypt, the population of 16th century England believed that they had to obey God to earn a place in the afterlife. Traditions

Amarna --- the missing evidence

were important and even though under Henry VIII, "God" was to be the same "God", the changes proposed in his worship caused uproar. Opposition to the changes was strong and violent, and the effects were felt across the entire country. Thousands of people were killed and the economic effects were widespread. Yet we are asked to believe that Akhenaten behaved in the same way as Henry VIII and no one even raised an objection? Akhenaten's reforms were in fact to be far more serious in that "God" himself was being abandoned. Yet the powerful priests of Amun at Karnak simply sat back and said nothing? Anyone who understands human nature will realise that religion is of great importance to people. Throughout history, and continuing today, men have fought and died for their beliefs. Pharaohs have been assassinated for much less than this! Yet the priests of Amun did nothing? They lost their power and wealth but did nothing? The people of Egypt did nothing? What was going to happen to the harvests if Amun was displeased? What would happen to them in the afterlife?

Interestingly, there are no records to show that the country's religion **did** change in any way. Foreign kings writing to Pharaoh make an occasional mention of Amun, but not one mention is made of the Aten. There are no contemporary records to show any disturbance, and the temples to Amun at Luxor and Karnak were not destroyed or altered to show a new god. "Restoration" Stelae from the reigns of Tutankhamen and Horemheb say that these Pharaohs "restored" the old faith, but more on that later.

There is no doubt that Akhenaten moved himself and his family to the new city of Akhetaten, and that this new city was the centre for the God Aten. Life in the new city, however, seems to have been totally dedicated to the worship of the God Aten, and few other activities are shown in reliefs or paintings anywhere. Tombs were built at Akhetaten for the nobles and officials, who moved to live there with Akhenaten, but their job titles show them to have been involved in the smooth running of the city or the care of

Chapter 2

the Royal family. Nothing has been found to suggest that Akhetaten was ever the capital city of Egypt. Akhetaten was clearly built by Akhenaten, for Akhenaten, and for the Aten. It was to be the "City of the Aten" not the capital of Egypt. As will be seen later, the only Pharaoh, who ever lived there permanently was Akhenaten himself. There is no evidence anywhere to suggest that life for the people of Egypt changed in any way at all.

So, if Akhenaten is now living out his new life in his new city, enjoying a new freedom, what is happening back in Thebes? Is Thebes falling into ruin? Are the priests of Amun unemployed? Is the population frantic with worry about their chances of a peaceful existence in the afterlife? Of course not! Life in the capital city of Egypt is continuing as before, and Amenhotep III lives on as Pharaoh.

Much has been written about long co-regency between Amenhotep III and his son, and there has been great disagreement over this. It seems quite clear, though, from the evidence that remains, that these two men, father and son, ruled together for almost the entire duration of Akhenaton's reign, with Amenhotep III dying only a short time before his son. (See chapter 5) There is a multitude of evidence to show that the two Pharaohs were alive together, whilst Akhenaten lived out his life at Akhetaten; and if we accept that a change of religion would have led to chaos then this has to have been so. Akhenaten, like most young men and sons of powerful fathers, wanted a place of his own.

Evidence is interesting. In modern times, trials by jury in Courts depend on evidence presented by each side. The Prosecution presents evidence of guilt and the Defence presents evidence of innocence. Often it is difficult deciding who has presented the most powerful arguments, but it only takes one piece of irrefutable evidence to settle the case. The Defence might provide alibi evidence – the defendant was somewhere else at the time of the crime; it might introduce witnesses or forensic evidence. But if the

Amarna --- the missing evidence

Prosecution produces CCTV images that show the defendant actually committing the crime then the case is proven. So it must be with research into Ancient Egypt. There may be arguments on both sides but it only takes one piece of evidence to prove or disprove an established theory. Read on.

Before we consider the evidence of the co-regency, let us consider the length of Akhenaten's reign. This is of vital importance in understanding the chronology. Books on the subject tell is that Akhenaten died sometime in year 17 of his reign. But is this really so? Where is the evidence? Most of the evidence for life at Akhetaten is found on the walls of the tombs built into the cliffs, and there are no paintings or reliefs in those tombs that can be dated beyond year 12. So where does this year 17 come from? It comes from wine jar! Yes, a wine jar! Wine in ancient Egyptian times was not stored in bottles with corks, but in clay jars. These jars were slightly porous, so it is unlikely that wine was stored in them for any great length of time. It is said that a wine jar was found at Akhetaten and inscribed: "Year 17" (but with the number 17, crossed out and number 1 written in its place). The implication is that this is a wine jar made in year 17 of one Pharaoh and is still in use when the new Pharaoh came to the throne. If the wine only had a short shelf life then year 17, of one Pharaoh must equate to year 1 of the next.

As often happens, we now see a classic example of "if not him, then who?" If the Pharaoh in year 17 is not Akhenaten, then who could it be? With no other evidence being offered, we are left with a history of Egypt and Pharaoh Akhenaten ruling for 17 years. This is a dangerous assumption. Wine may not have been stored in the jars for any length of time, but the jars were valuable, and it is quite likely that they were reused several times. One very well-documented wine jar was found at Akhetaten and its inscription was: Regnal year 17: wine of the Estate of Neb-maat-re. This jar provides valuable evidence in two ways. It clearly belonged to Amenhotep III and the wine was bottled in his reign. So, either Amenhotep III was alive during

Chapter 2

Akhenaten's reign or the jar was very old and still in use. If there was no co-regency, then the wine jar, must have been at least 21 years old when Amenhotep III died, as he probably reigned for 38/39 years. The jar must also have been moved to Akhetaten from Thebes, and still have survived for possibly the length of Akhenaton's reign only to be discarded in the sand as the city was deserted. This seems unlikely. It is much more likely that Amenhotep III's entourage brought the jar to Akhetaten during one of Amenhotep III's visits. If we discount the flimsy evidence of the wine jar then there is no evidence that Akhenaten ruled for more than 12 years. As he moved to Akhetaten in years six, the city was not completed before year 8 and was occupied for not much more than 4 years. More on this later.

Wine jar dockets were found at Akhetaten with Years 28 and 30 written on them. These dates cannot refer to the reign of Akhenaten, who did not rule for so long. The dockets in question must have been written in the reign of Amenhotep III, who was the only king of the period to rule for this length of time. The conclusion of the British archaeologists Pendlebury and Fairman was that if the jars had reached Amarna full of wine then the contents must have been at least fourteen years old when they arrived. As wine is presumed not to keep long in permeable pottery jars in a warm climate, they argue that it is most likely that Years 28 and 30 of Amenhotep III were nearer to Year 6 of Akhenaten when Akhetaten was first occupied.

With this chronology and accepting that Akhenaten died in or soon after his year 12 it is clear to see that Amenhotep III was alive throughout most of his son's reign. Future Kings' Lists make no mention of Amenhotep IV/Akhenaten, and of course they wouldn't if his rule was contemporaneous with his father's. Remember the situation with Hatshepsut and Tuthmoses III? She did not take the throne ***before*** her step-son, or rule ***after*** him. She had no place in the chronology

Amarna --- the missing evidence

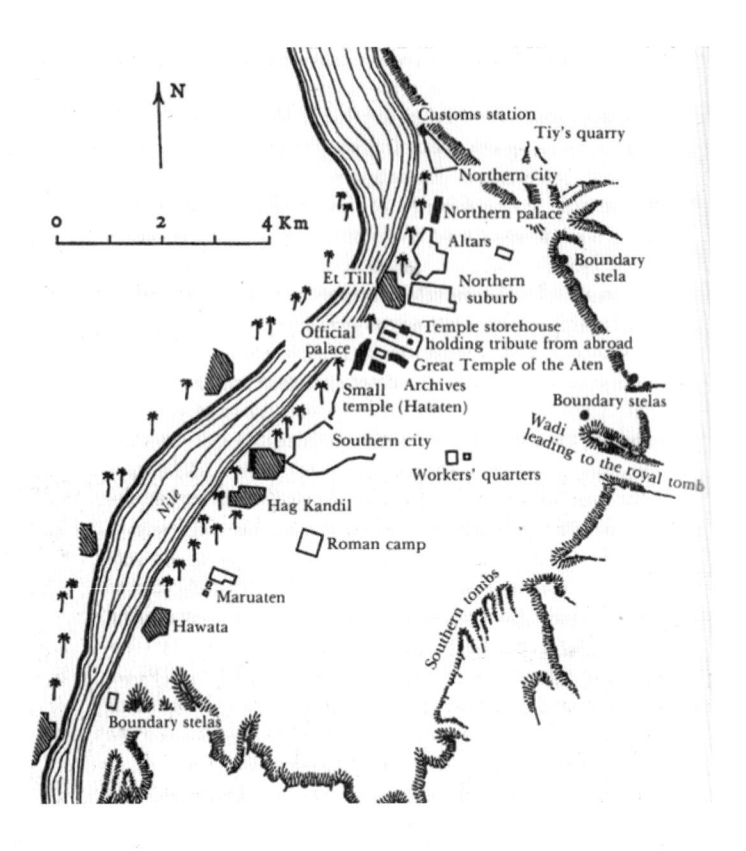

Fig 2.8. Plan of Akhetaten.

Let's look for a moment at the layout of Akhetaten, and then the Nobles who lived there with Akhenaten. The City of the Aten was created in the desert area of Egypt on the east bank of the River Nile. Akhetaten was made up of temples, social facilities such as grain silos and bakeries, palaces and common mud-brick homes, as well as a number of other public buildings. The city is quite amazing if one considers that it was built in a few years and inhabited by the Royal Family for such short space of time. The workers' village was not well built. Excavations in the area have shown that two types

Chapter 2

of mud bricks were made. In the first flush of enthusiasm, good quality mud bricks were created, made from Nile mud mixed with gravel. The workers then appear to have been left to finish their homes, and used marl which was closer to hand. The buildings do not appear to have been decorated, and there were no wells serving the village. Water had to be collected from the river Nile some two miles away. Akhenaten either did not care about the living conditions of the workers, or he was making the best of a bad job. This was not a good choice of site for a new city.

Fig 2.9. Mud bricks at Akhetaten.

The City shows a remarkable lack of Government Offices. Offices have been excavated, but if this was to have been the Capital of Egypt, the administrative centre of the most powerful country in the world at the time,

Amarna --- the missing evidence

then much is lacking. There is overriding evidence that life in the city was one long duty of worship to the Aten and a celebration of the royal family. The tombs of the nobles were decorated with scenes of Aten worship or of the Royal Family taking food. Images of the tomb owner receiving rewards from Akhenaten also feature prominently. Only in the last two tombs to be built do we see any reference to International Relationships. These will be examined in detail later.

Chapter 2

To conclude:

Version 1 (the Established version)

In year 6 of his reign, Pharaoh Amenhotep IV changed his name.

He moved to a new city he had built in the desert. The city was called Akhetaten.

Akhenaten ruled alone for 17 years.

He abandoned Thebes and the old god Amun, and established his favourite god Aten as the new god of Egypt.

The population of Egypt was quite happy with this.

Version 2 (My version)

In year 6 of his reign, Pharaoh Amenhotep IV changed his name.

He moved to a new city he had built in the desert. The city was called Akhetaten.

His father Amenhotep III ruled Egypt from Thebes.

Akhenaton lived out his life at Akhetaten with his wife and family, worshiping his chosen god.

Akhenaten ruled for little more than 12 years.

The population of Egypt was quite happy with this.

You decide

Chapter 3

Who lived in Akhetaten?

"I know the answer! The answer lies within the heart of all mankind! The answer is twelve? I think I'm in the wrong building."

--- **Charles M. Schulz**

So far we know that in Year 6 of his reign, Amenhotep IV changed his name to Akhenaten and moved with his wife Nefertiti and two, possibly three daughters to his new City, Akhetaten. But who moved with him? The Court Officials? The Palace entourage? Let's see.

Most of the information known of the important people at Akhetaten comes from their tombs. In the cliffs of the city two sets of tombs were built, known today as the Northern Tombs and the Southern Tombs. The layout of the City, shown in the previous chapter, shows where these tombs were situated. Most of the tombs were unfinished, and some have been so badly damaged we do not know who they were built for; but there is much information to be gathered from the remaining tombs. There are some remarkable scenes still visible today, and many others that were carefully recorded in the 19th century.

So, who are these nobles? Being Pharaoh is a bit like being the head of a modern government. The style of government might be democratic or the King/President might be a dictator, but he cannot rule alone. He needs experts in different areas and he needs their undying loyalty. Except in a few cases, the "nobles" at Akhetaten were *not* the trusted nobles from Thebes. Many were unknown before the move. Before we look at the tombs

Amarna --- the missing evidence

individually, we need to understand that the numbering of the tombs is a relatively modern system. The people who lived at Akhetaten would not have known the tombs by these numbers, and they were not built in the order we appear to see today.

The tombs seem to have been mass produced. The internal decoration is revealing, but there is none of the originality and beauty seen in earlier tombs in Egypt. Apart from the Royal Tomb, and the tombs of the nobles known to us as tombs 1 and 2, all of the building work on the tombs was abandoned by year 9. As tombs 1 and 2 were built later than the rest, we would gain more from them by looking at them last. So, who were the nobles who moved to Akhetaten with their Pharaohs?

In the Northern tombs, tomb number 3 we meet **Ahmose**. His title is ***"First Servant of Akhenaten"*** – and clearly an elderly man who has been Akhenaten's servant since the latter was a young man. This gives us a clue as to the background of some of Akhenaten's followers. Ahmose professes no skills which might help govern the new city – just undying loyalty to his young master" *I have completed a lifetime of happiness, being in the following of the Good God wherever he went, being loved when I was his attendant"*.

On the Lintel of the outer door of his tomb are the words:

Tendering adoration to the living Aten and kissing the ground to the Good God by the seal bearer of the King of Lower Egypt, the sole companion, the attendant of the Lord of the Two Lands, the favourite of the Good God, one beloved of his lord every day, the true king's scribe, his beloved, the steward of the house of Akhenaten, overseer of the front hall of the Lord of the Two Lands, Ahmose, justified, possessor of holiness..

The texts are stereotyped in each tomb – praise offered to the god Aten and just as much praise offered to the Pharaoh Akhenaten. The interesting part of the texts is shown on the outer door jambs:

Chapter 3

" --- rejoicing daily and the seeing of his ***handsome face*** every day ---"
Handsome face? Akhenaten? This is either an extreme example of flattery or the representations of Akhenaten in the tombs are in no way accurate.

Fig 3.1 Scene from Ahmose's tomb.

In **Tomb 4** *"The Greatest of Seers of the Aten"* **Meryre** I carved out scenes of the Royal Family and a great many images of himself receiving rewards of golden collars from his Pharaoh. Pharaoh spoke to him on this occasion with the following words:

Here I am present to promote thee to be Chief Seer of the Disk of the Sun, in the temple of the Sun of the city of Akhetaten. Be thou such, according to thy wish, for thou was my servant, who was obedient to the new teaching. Besides thee, none has done this. My heart is full of contentment because of this; therefore I give thee this office, saying, Eat of the nourishment of Pharaoh thy lord in the temple of the Sun.

Amarna --- the missing evidence

Meryre's tomb is better preserved than many, although there is much damage, some caused soon after the city was abandoned, but much more in later times. The Copts plastered over sections of the walls and carved niches wherever they were needed, and more modern day visitors, namely dealers in antiquities, also added to the mutilation. There are still some beautiful scenes visible, not least the one shown below, showing the procession of the King and Queen. Luckily the scene of Meryre being rewarded by Akhenaton is well preserved.

Ahmose was not the only one to speak of his Pharaoh's beauty. In Meryre's tomb there is the inscription:

--- *he says "Health to Waenre" the **beautiful** child of the Aten.*

Tomb **5** was built for **Pentu *"Chief Physician"*.** Pentu's tomb showed again one of the many mass produced scenes, that of the tomb owner being rewarded by the King with golden collars. This is a scene which was probably in every tomb – it is a scene that was visible in every undamaged tomb at the end of the 19th century. What was the meaning of the scene? Was it designed to show the generosity of Pharaoh? If so, then who was to see it? There is no evidence of anyone touring the tombs – hardly anyone came to Akhetaten anyway.

Fig 3.2. Scene from Meryre's tomb.

Chapter 3

Was it designed to make the tomb owner feel important? This seems more likely. Something to show what a good man he was, and that Akhenaten thought highly of him. It could certainly bring loyalty. Pentu is one of the few nobles to survive the move to Akhetaten and continue in office under Tutankhamen. He became "Southern Vizier" under that King.

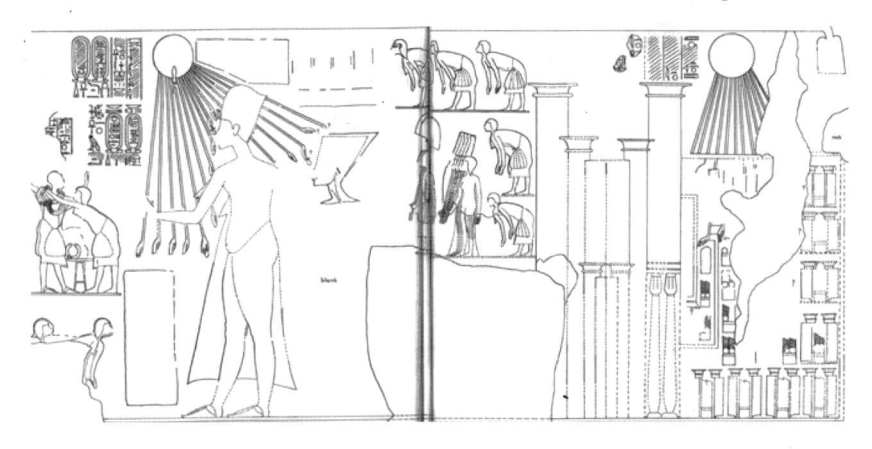

Fig 3.3. Pentu rewarded with Gold Collars.

Tomb 6 was built for the noble was **Penhesy,** *"First servant of the Aten"* in the house of the Aten in Akhetaten. Second prophet of the Lord of the Two Lands Neferkheprure-waenre (Akhenaten). Overseer of the double granary of the Aten in Akhetaten. Overseer of cattle of the Aten. Panhesy's tomb shows the second of the mass produced scenes – the scene showing the Royal Family offering to the Aten. Tables are full of delicious foods and the family offers this to their god. He was a high priest, and his tomb is quite ornate compared to the others.

Panhesy tells us of his origins: *" adoration to you, my god, who built me, the one who fated good things for me --- who caused me to be powerful when I had been poor."* Panhesy is not a long standing official, then. He was a poor man promoted to his position by Akhenaten. In Panhesy's tomb we are introduced to his family, who are shown sitting at a table. His son stands beside his chair and two daughters stand beside their mother. His wife is named as "the housewife Iabka."

Fig 3.4 Penhesy's tomb.

Chapter 3

So far, then, in the first four tombs, there is no sign of any official needed to rule a great country like Egypt. All we have are junior nobles who are concerned with the well being of the Royal Family or the Aten. But where are the important officials? There are more tombs to examine, but to date no-one has uncovered any nobles who might have been involved in the ***government of Egypt***. Why not? Because Egypt is still being ruled by Amenhotep III in Thebes.

We now move to the Southern Tombs and find that **Tomb 7** was built for the *"Cupbearer"* **Parennefer** His other Titles were The King's Cup Bearer, Washer of the King's Hands, Chief Craftsman, Overseer of All the Works in the Mansion of the Aten We know something of Parennefer, in that he tells us he is the son of Aupia, who was Chief Craftsman of Amenhotep III. His tomb scenes include one showing him being rewarded by his Pharaoh. Yet another tomb and no important powers. Parennefer's tombs, like the others, was unfinished and Parennefer was actually buried at Thebes in Theban Tomb 188. He may have been known to Akhenaten before the move to Akhetaten, as the building of the shrine to the Aten at Karnak is attributed to him. A good, loyal servant, then – but no international diplomat.

Fig 3.5. Parennefer rewarded with Gold Collars.

Amarna --- the missing evidence

Tomb 8 belonged to *"The Chamberlain"* **Tutu**. Chamberlain of the Lord of the Two Lands, the overseer of all that the Lord of the Two Lands, Overseer of gold and silver of the Lord of the Two Lands, treasurer of Aten in the house of the Aten in Akhetaten, the district overseer, chief servitor of Neferkheperure-Waenre (Akhenaten) in the house of Aten in Akhetaten. Compare the standard "reward" scene of Tutu. The same imagery is used on the others we have seen. *Collars.* Where golden collars a symbol of the new religion? Did wearing gold around the neck represent the power of the sun in some way? These collars were clearly highly prized and the nobles who received them clearly rejoiced at the great honour bestowed on them. Their Pharaoh was doing what all good Pharaohs do – acting as the go-between between man and his God.

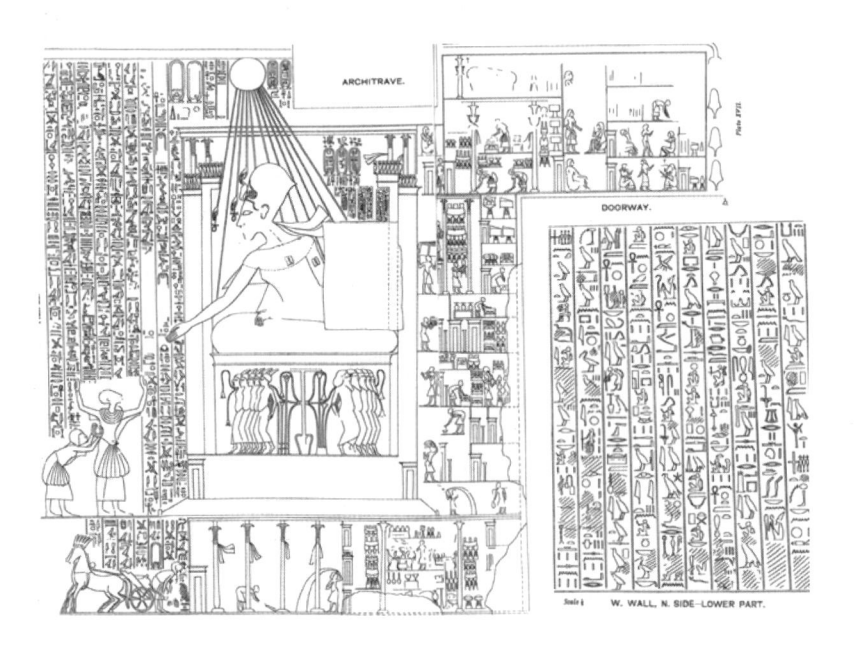

Fig 3.6. Tutu rewarded with Gold Collars

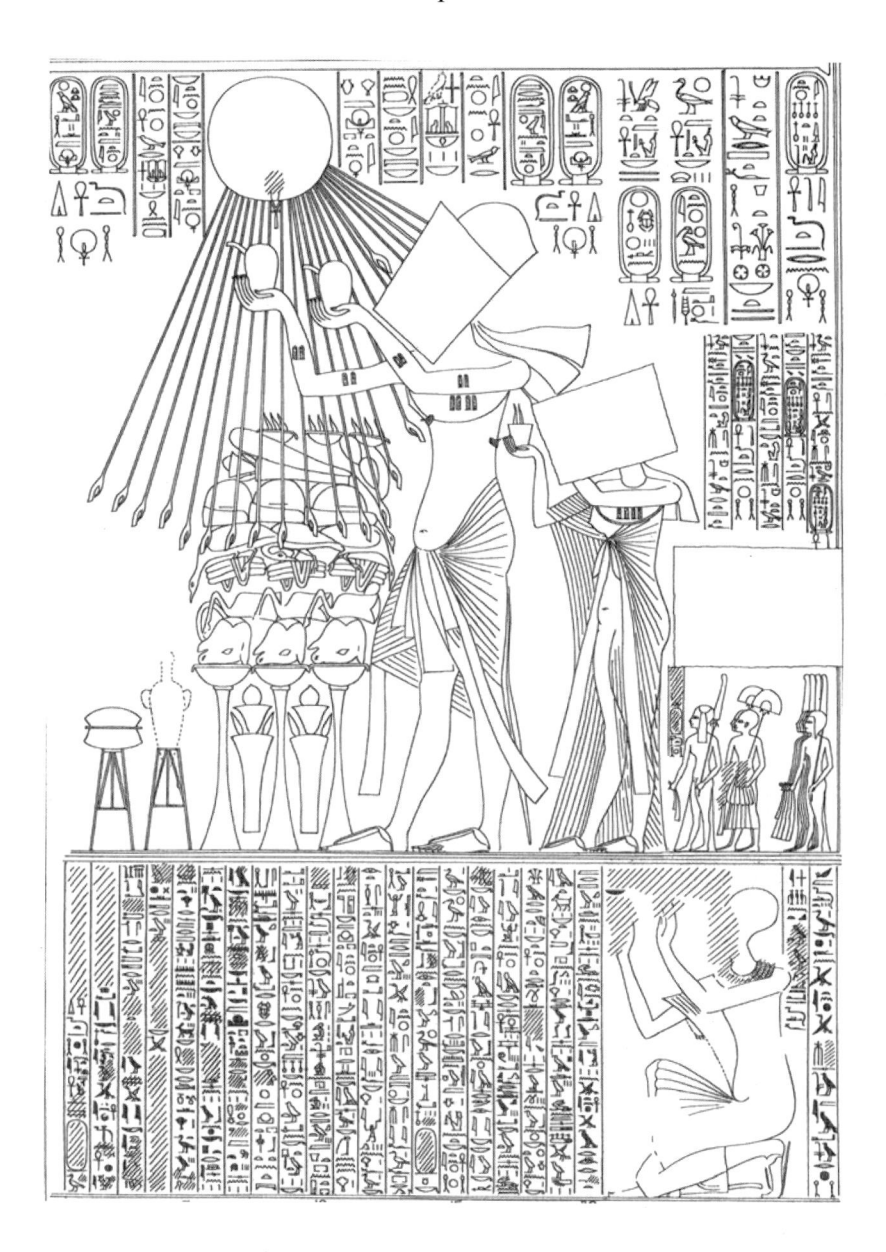

Fig 3.7. Scene of worship in Tutu's tomb.

Amarna --- the missing evidence

Tomb 9. gets a little more interesting, as at last we find someone with real work to do! **Mahu** *"Chief of the Police at Akhetaten"* Mahu is shown doing his work, and then reporting to the Vizier in Akhetaten. He is also shown travelling in a chariot inspecting a squad of the Police. Mahu's tomb shows the reward scene and the worship scene.

Mahu's tomb also shows the second mass produced scene – that of the Royal family offering to the Aten. This scene appears in most tombs and Tutu's is a good example.

Fig 3.8. Scene of worship from Mahu's tomb.

Chapter 3

In **Tomb 10** we have information about its owner, **Apy** is also known from Thebes. Apy came from a prominent Memphite family, and was related to Ramose who was City Overseer of Memphis. **Apy** served Akhenaten when he was known as Amenhotep IV. He is **"The Chief Steward"**. So **Apy**, like Parennefer was related to an important man. So why didn't the "important men" themselves move to Akhetaten? Presumably Amenhotep III still needed them. Apy's tomb shows the worship scene.

Tomb 11 belonged to Ramose Scribe of Recruits, General of the Lord of the Two Lands, the king's scribe, Steward of the house of Nebmaatre (Amenhotep III). Now why would Amenhotep III need a Steward if he was dead? There is not much left to read in Ramose's tomb, but it is reasonable to suppose the same scenes of worship and reward would have been visible in the past.

Tomb 12. is really interesting. **Nakhtpaaten** *"Vizier"*. Hereditary prince, count, sealbearer, overseer of the city and vizier, overseer of the work projects in Akhet-Aten. The dictionary definition of the word Vizier is: *The chief minister of Egypt answerable only to the Pharaoh. He was responsible for the day-to-day running of the country.* ... The important word here being "country". **Nakhtpaaten** was clearly only Vizier of *Akhetaten* – he says so. The wording "Hereditary prince" is of greatest interest. Is this man a member of the royal family? The name "Nakht" means "Strong One".

The few surviving texts in the tomb refer to this man as Nakht, and as "Pa-Aten" means " the house of Aten" this would seem to be a later addition, not part of the name given to him at his birth.

Tomb 13 was built for **Neferkhepre-her-sekheper** *"Mayor of Akhetaten"*. Another official at Akhetaten. Nothing to do with running the country. This tomb was cut and almost complete but the inscriptions were not carved before it was abandoned. The few texts from the entrance speak of his devotion to Akhenaten.

Amarna --- the missing evidence

Another interesting tomb **is Tomb 14,** that of **May** ***"Fan-bearer on the Kings right hand".*** He describes himself as Count, the seal-bearer of the king of Upper and Lower Egypt, the sole companion, the true king's scribe, General of the Lord of the Two Lands, Steward of the house of 'Pacifying the Aten', Scribe of Recruits, Steward of Waenre (Akhenaten) in Heliopolis, Overseer of the cattle of the house of Re in Heliopolis, Overseer of all works of the king, Fan-bearer on the right hand of the king. In the inscriptions in his tomb May writes: *"I am a servant of his creating--- he has doubled my favours --- I was a poor man on both my father's and mother's side – but the ruler built me up, he caused me to develop, he fed me by means of his Ka when I was without property."* Another noble raised from no-where to serve at Akhetaten.

Tomb 15 belonged to **Suty** *"Standard-Bearer "*of the company of Neferkheperure-Waenre (Akhenaten). We know little of him because his tomb, as with the tomb of **Neferkhepre-her-sekheper** was not finished and was not inscribed.

The occupants of Tombs 16, 17 and 18 are unknown, but in **Tomb 19** we have another poor man made good ***"The treasurer"* Sutau.** He tells us *" I was a poor man but the ruler built me up".* The tomb was not finished or fully inscribed, so we know little of this man or his work. Satau was "Treasurer to the Lord of the Two Lands". He does not claim to be Treasurer of Egypt.

The owners of tombs 20 to 22 are unknown. In **Tomb 23** we meet the ***"King's Scribe and Steward", Any.*** Any tells us how grateful he is to Akhenaten for providing him with a "good funeral" and describes himself as "*Royal Scribe; Scribe of Offerings of the Lord of the Two Lands; Scribe of Offerings of the Aten; Steward of the House of Aakheperure (Amenhotep II)"* The most interesting feature of Any's tomb is his shrine where we meet the family. His wife was Awy. Six small stelae were found in Any's tomb each

Chapter 3

with the name of a scribe. These scribes were Pakha, Nebawai, Anymen, Tchay, Ptahmay andd Iay.

Tomb 24 was built for *"The Commander"* **Pa-aten-em-heb**. Only the entrance is carved for the chief scribe and general in Akhetaten. This gives us food for thought. The nobles at Akhetaten were, on the whole, unknown before their elevation. Even assuming that Pa-aten-em-heb was an unknown he must have been at least twenty years old surely. He is a "Commander". So, assuming that he was born at least twenty years before the building of Akhetaten, how does he come to have the name "Aten" in his name? Apart from Nakht Pa-Aten, and the royal family, no other person at Akhetaten carried the god's name "Aten" in their name. We know that Akhenaten changed his name to feature that of the god, and it must be logical to think that Pa-aten-em-heb was not this man's birth name.

It is possible that this is Horemheb, future Pharaoh. Looking at events in a holistic way, this does seem quite likely. Horemheb's influence is felt throughout the late 18th dynasty and he would have been a likely candidate to move to Akhetaten with the young Pharaoh. His titles are similar "King's scribe, General of the Lord of the Two Lands, Steward of the Lord of the Two Lands".

One man who *definitely* moved to Akhenaten with the royal family was **Aye**. Known as the *"God's Father Aye"* we will examine his role later, but he appears here as a "Father" figure. Amenhotep III cannot be with his son all the time, so did Aye take on the challenge? His **tomb was no 25.** Aye describes himself as "The favourite of the good god, Fan-bearer on the right of the King, True King's Scribe, God's Father. The commander of all the horses of his Person, The confidante throughout the entire land"

In the tomb we also see images of Mutnodjme, Nefertiti's Sister. Her figure is lost, but her two dwarfs Hemetniswerneheh and Mutef-Pre are visible. This sister is of interest in that we have here another example of

Amarnan name changes. Mutnodjme means "Sweet Mother". It is not really credible that a mother looking at her new-born baby daughter should call her "Sweet Mother"! Mutnodjme is shown at Akhetaten as nurse-maid to the Royal Children –their Aunt, and the name clearly fits this role. This could be an example of a foreign name being changed to an Egyptian one. More of

that later.

Fig 3.9. From the tomb of Aye Reward scene showing Aye and his wife Tiiy receiving gifts from Akhenaten, Nefertiti, Merytaten, Meketaten and Ankhesenpaaten.

These then are the nobles whose tombs were all left unfinished around year 9 of their Pharaoh Akhenaten. We have seen how some simply moved back to Thebes – one even to become Pharaoh himself – and many others may have followed but we have not been able to identify their tombs.

Chapter 3

Let us now go back to the two remaining tombs, those of Huya and Meryre II. These two tombs were dug at a later date – probably around year 9 - and were still being decorated in year 12. They will be discussed in great detail in chapter 5, but for now let us think more about the men themselves.

Tomb 1 was built for 1 **Huya**, whose title was *"Chief Steward of Queen Tiy"* Huya was the Steward to Queen Tiy, and Superintendent of the Royal Harem. He is shown at the entrance to the tomb with his family, Queen Tiy and two princesses, but the rest of the tomb is covered in images of Akhenaten decorating Huya and worshipping the sun god. In Huya's tomb we meet Beketaten, Akhenaten's younger sister. It would seem as if Huya's entire family moved to Akhetaten with him as scenes show his sister (probably wife) Wenher and his mother Tuy. Mention is also made of his sisters Nebet and Kherput.

3.10. Huya rewarded with Gold Collars.

Amarna --- the missing evidence

In **Tomb 2** the scenes show its owner, ***"Overseer of the Royal Quarters"* Meryre II.** As with the tomb of Huya (tomb 1) this was one of the last of the tombs to be built and provide evidence of the aftermath of Akhenaten's reign. Meryre II was Nefertiti's steward, and this tomb gives good evidence about events at the end of Akhenaten's reign. Much more about this tomb later.

The tombs, then, tell us of the important people who lived with Akhenaten in his new city. Few had any experience and apart from mass produced texts and images, few seemed to have much allegiance to the Aten. A few other names have been unearthed as the city has been explored. A shawabti figure was found bearing the name "**Hat**", whose title was "The Deputy." And another was found with the name **Py**, a court lady. A house was discovered that belonged to the Builder, **Hatiay**, and another belonging to the Chief Builder **Maanakhtef.** Other houses belonged to **Ranofer**, the Chief Charioteer and the High Priest of Re, **Pawah**. Ranofer's house was built during the reign of Akhenaten's mysterious successor and the cartouches uncovered there provide valuable information as to the identity of this Pharaoh.

From a relief in the granite quarry at Aswan we know that the Chief Sculptor Bek was with Akhenaten at Akhetaten. He was the son of Amenhotep III's chief sculptor Men. Bek plays an important role in changing the Art style. So what do we make of all this? Obviously a great many more people lived at Akhetaten, but the most important were the men who were granted tombs. And you have now met them all.

There is no-one of any real importance named in the tombs. The men we see there were just puppets who would do whatever they are asked in return for a few gold collars and a good funeral. Who is running the country? Where are the International Diplomats? The tax collectors? The men needed to run a great nation like Egypt.

Chapter 3

Note:

Apart from the Author's own photos, the illustrations in this chapter are taken from: de Garis Davies, N., (1903-1908). *The Rock Tombs of El Amarna.* London: Egypt Exploration Society

To conclude:

Version 1 (the Established version)

Akhetaten was the Capital City of Egypt.

The Government of Egypt moved to Akhetaten.

Akhenaten ruled Egypt from this city, and the country prospered.

Nothing changed from the years of rule from Thebes

Version 2 (My version)

Akhetaten was Akhenaten's new city. He lived there with his wife and family.

Akhetaten was governed by Akhenaten, helped by a new generation of "Nobles".

No-one complained about an enforced change in religion – because there was no change.

The Country prospered.

Nothing changed from the years of rule from Thebes.

You decide.

Chapter 4

Art at Akhetaten –
Or - what did Akhenaten really look like?

"People often say that 'beauty is in the eye of the beholder,' and I say that the most liberating thing about beauty is realizing that you are the beholder. This empowers us to find beauty in places where others have not dared to look, including inside ourselves." --- **Salma Hayek**

When the city of Akhetaten was first discovered, the scenes on the walls of the tombs caused great concern. Egyptologists and Explorers were used to seeing images of Pharaohs and their families in a traditional, formal pose. The kings were shown as serene, stately heads of state and it was clearly important that the people should see them as unemotional. Emotion would give the impression of a weak man, not the kind of person you would want in charge of a powerful country like Egypt. Not the kind of king the gods would listen to. Pharaoh should be seen as handsome, strong, well proportioned and perfect in every way.

At Akhetaten we see a complete change. The royal family are suddenly shown as elongated, deformed figures. Their heads are egg shaped and their bodies are very ugly and angled. Akhenaten is shown with rounded, feminine hips and a pot belly. So great was the change in style it was initially thought that these must be different people. Pharaoh is not seen as perfect and without emotion. Quite the opposite in fact. He is seen as a very strange, emotional figure, often kissing his wife Nefertiti or one of his daughters.

Amarna --- the missing evidence

Instead of the image of a powerful Pharaoh, ready to deal with any problems that come along, we see Akhenaten sitting eating a meal with his family or playing with his children. Hardly the image of the all powerful ruler of a great country. But then, he wasn't the all powerful ruler of a great country, was he?

With this strange and deformed appearance, Akhenaten quickly became one of the most fascinating Pharaoh's of all time. It has been speculated that Akhenaten was really a woman or that he suffered from Marfan's Syndrome, a genetic disorder that affects the skeleton and muscles. Yet Akhenaten does not appear to have a muscular problem.

Fig 4.1. Head of Akhenaten showing elongated skull and breasts.

His wife and his children were depicted with the same body shape and deformities, and it was assumed that his daughters inherited his disorder.

Chapter 4

A disease might pass from father to daughters, but would it pass from a man to his wife? Hardly! So perhaps Nefertiti did not want to appear left out.

Perhaps he was born sickly and deformed with this strange shaped skull, thin limbs, and prominent hips, breasts, and paunch. A Yale University doctor who analysed images of Akhenaten for an annual conference at the University of Maryland School of Medicine has concluded that Akhenaten's female form was due to a genetic mutation that caused his body to convert more male hormones to female hormones than needed. He was, however, only looking at images.

These are just a few of the explanations that have been offered about Akhenaten's strange appearance. He was really a woman, he was elongated and deformed and he suffered from Marfan's Syndrome. But is any of this true? What did Akhenaten really look like?

Before we discuss Akhenaten's appearance, another famous figure should be considered. Pablo Picasso. Fortunately for him, cameras had been invented and a photograph confirms his real appearance. Yet from his self-portraits we might consider that Picasso suffered from the same complaints as Akhenaten! The similarities in Art styles are quite remarkable, but fortunately the photograph makes it quite clear that this is exactly it: an "Art Style." Picasso did not have two eyes and his nose was not grossly oversized.

Art was revolutionised during the Akhetaten Period, and the new representations are due to a complete change in style. The art of Akhenaten's time featured a new realism, which was perhaps created to form a closer link between the king and his people.

This closer link features strongly throughout Akhenaten's reign, and, as we have seen, he even selected his Nobles from a pool of unknown, ordinary people. Images now showed intimacy and featured the naturalness of the surroundings including vegetation and animals

Fig 4.2 Pablo Picasso. Self-Portrait.

.The royal women played a more prominent role in art as well. In the Art at Akhetaten there are numerous images of the king and his royal family, adored from above by the Aten. The informal poses in these images is also quite new. Nothing like this had ever been seen before – and was never seen again when the city of Akhetaten was deserted.

Fig 4.3 is just one example of the new art style. Akhenaten and Nefertiti are shown of equal size which was unheard of before. The Queen was always shown as a much smaller figure. The royal daughters are shown in action, not standing demurely beside their parents. They are behaving in a

Chapter 4

much more natural way, as young children and babies would behave, and their parents are responding in a natural way as well.

Fig 4.3. The happy family.

Amarna --- the missing evidence

Other images show the Royal Couple conducting everyday activities, rewarding Nobles or offering to their god. Instead of appearing as strong, perfect specimens of manhood, Akhenaten was shown with this elongated face and neck, protruding chin, sunken chest, obvious breasts, pot belly, wide hips and thighs, and spindly arms and legs. It would seem that the artists were attempting to portray Akhenaten with brutal naturalness, to the extent that the images became caricatures. The master sculptor, Bek, who was responsible for this change in art style, claimed to have been taught by Akhenaten himself. Whether this means that Akhenaten actually taught him his trade or merely told him what he wanted the art to look like Bek does not say, but the latter is probably more likely. Since such a depiction of Akhenaten could only have been created with his approval, we must take it that he had a motive for this.

He called himself Wa-en-Re, or "The Unique One of Re," thus emphasising the fact that he was not like anyone else, and he also placed a lot of emphasis on the unique nature of his god, Aten. As we have seen, his nobles speak of his beauty, and this deserves consideration. No other Pharaoh has so many comments made about their incredibly beautiful appearance, yet this Pharaoh has gone to great lengths to appear ugly. Why? This was the Pharaoh who devoted his life to a new god, so it would seem most likely that this change in art style was connected to the new religion.

In the second half of Akhenaten's reign, the style changed abruptly again, probably because a new master sculptor, Tuthmose, took over. The remains of Tuthmose's workshop have provided us with an incredible insight into the way the artists created their work. Tuthmose had a style which was decidedly more realistic than Bek's. He produced some of the finest art in Egyptian history, and his portraits are also probably some of the most accurate images of the Akhetaten family in existence.

Akhenaten's daughters all display the strange elongation in their

Chapter 4

skulls and as both Akhenaten's and Tutankhamen's skulls show an elongation, it is almost certainly an accurate depiction. We have actual evidence in these skulls and proof that the head shapes are unusual. Neither Mummy shows breasts, swollen hips, legs out of proportion or any other physical abnormality. This really settles the argument. Akhenaten was of normal shape but with an elongated skull. The way he chose to present himself must have been due to his religion – and was something else which must surely have angered the Priests of Amun.

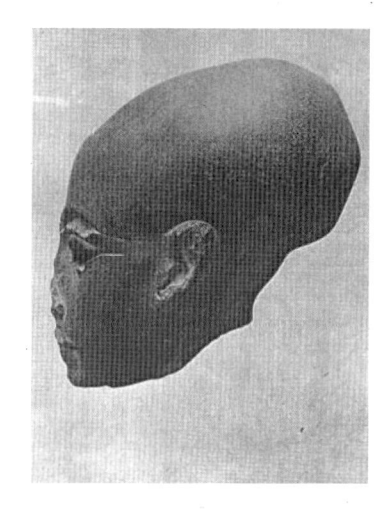

Fig 4.4 Amarna head shapes.

One statue reveals more than others. It is a statue of Akhenaten made in the 9th year of his reign, standing beside his wife, Nefertiti. (Fig 4.5)

Amarna --- the missing evidence

Fig 4.5. Akhenaten in the 9th year of his reign, with Nefertiti.

Although the figure of Akhenaten does not appear to be that of a powerful Pharaoh, the body is in much better proportion than was seen over the previous three years. Breasts are not visible, the hips are not swollen, and

Chapter 4

the legs appear quite well built. Nefertiti shows breasts, but not her husband. She is shown as shorter than her husband, but only proportionately shorter – as most women are slightly shorter than men anyway. They look to be an ordinary couple in every way, but not really like a Pharaoh and his wife. Take a look at a close up of Nefertiti's Head. Is this really the most beautiful woman in the world? Is this really the woman whose face is shown on the famous bust? - the face bears no similarity to the famous bust of Nefertiti on display in Berlin! Sculpted at Akhetaten, this statue of the royal couple shows a more conventional style. It was found at Akhetaten and raises some interesting questions.

Fig 4.6. Close up of the head of Nefertiti.

Amarna --- the missing evidence

Under Tuthmose, two-dimensional art also changed. These changes are important as events at the time must also have been changing. Take for example the relief of Akhenaten and Nefertiti shown on the next page.

Fig 4.7 . Heads of Akhenaten and Nefertiti.

Fig 4.7 shows Akhenaten and Nefertiti. Akhenaten, the face on the left is very different from the early representation of him. Here he is shown with a smaller mouth, larger eyes, and softer features. He looks more subdued and serene than the earlier images. Nefertiti has also changed. She no longer looks like Akhenaten, but has a distinctive face of her own.

So what are we to make of all this? Was Akhenaten deformed? Should we be taking what we see in the tombs at Akhetaten at face value? Or should we be thinking more sensibly. He looks like a woman in many scenes, yet he fathered six daughters!

Art at Akhetaten is often considered to be just *one* Art form. Amarna Art. It is really *two* Art Forms. The first under the Artist and

Chapter 4

Sculptor Bek shows Akhenaten and the Royal Family in a harsh, elongated style – grossly distorted and in no way "normal."

When Tuthmose takes over, the Art Style softens and although Akhenaten clearly makes the same "back to nature, one of the people" statement, this is a little less jarring on the eye. From forensic evidence, elongated heads are quite likely to be genuine. Dolichocephalism, or elongated head syndrome is not uncommon and can be caused by breach birth or even premature birth. In many cultures this is considered a mark of beauty as well.

The majority of the population of Egypt could not read. Today we hear about our leaders from newspapers, journals, the internet, TV or radio, but in 1350BC the only way the people of Egypt got to know their Pharaoh was by looking at his statues. Pharaoh protected his people, and acted as a go-between to the gods – he had to be someone they respected and could rely on. Could anyone rely on a Pharaoh who looked as this one did? Could they rely on a distorted effeminate Pharaoh to protect them and speak to the gods on their behalf? It seems very unlikely! But then they did not have to rely on him. Akhenaten had removed himself from the seat of power to a remote city in the desert. Akhenaten only ever appears in the images on the walls of the tombs of the nobles in three situations. He is only ever shown:

1. Worshiping the Aten.
2. Rewarding his nobles with gold collars.
3. Relaxing with his family.

He is entirely preoccupied with the Aten and his family. It seems unlikely that his instructions to Bek, to change the art form, were inspired by any motive other than his religion. If we could only understand the religion fully, then we might understand these reasons.

Amarna --- the missing evidence

Apart from the elongated skull which clearly ran in the family (see Tutankhamen's skull below) it is unlikely that Akhenaten was in any way deformed physically. Mentally it is much harder to decide.

To conclude:

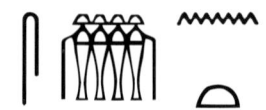

Version 1 (the Established version)

Akhenaten was born sickly and deformed with an elongated skull, thin limbs, and prominent hips, breasts, and paunch.
Akhenaten was really a woman.
Akhenaten suffered from Marfan's syndrome.
Akhenaten had a genetic mutation that caused his body to convert more male hormones to female hormones than needed.

Version 2 (My version)

The new artists and sculptors employed at Akhetaten were attempting to portray Akhenaten as "at one" with his religion.

The master sculptor, Bek, claimed to have been taught by Akhenaten himself.

Akhenaten called himself Wa-en-Re, or "The Unique One of Re," thus emphasising the fact that he was not like anyone else, and he also placed a lot of emphasis on the unique nature of his god, Aten.

You decide.

𓊪𓄿𓇋𓀀

Chapter 5

The Co-Regency

"The whole world is in revolt. Soon there will be only five Kings left--the King of England, the King of Spades, The King of Clubs, the King of Hearts, and the King of Diamonds." --- **King Farouk of Egypt**

So much has been written about the co-regency of Amenhotep III and Akhenaten that it is not my intention to reproduce it all in one chapter. Views have been presented on both sides to show that Akhenaten ruled alone for 17 years or that he ruled alongside his father for 12 years then 5 years on his own. My findings show that there was a full co-regency of some 11/12 years and that Akhenaten died soon after his father – outliving him by no more than two years. I have presented the most important evidence here. Evidence that really cannot be disputed, and which also gives the most sensible version of events.

Before we look at the evidence to support my findings, let's step back and look at the situation from a purely human point of view. In Akhenaten we see a Pharaoh who hides himself away in a remote desert city. He portrays himself as an emotional, effeminate man whose only interests in life are his god and his family. He never leaves this new city, and he surrounds himself with unknown, untrained "nobles." He cannot intercede between the old gods and the people as he does not recognise them any more.

We have been told that this Pharaoh ruled Egypt for seventeen years, and yet no-one noticed that Pharaoh had disappeared to the remote desert city known as Akhetaten? No-one noticed that Pharaoh was no longer

Amarna --- the missing evidence

the strong, impassioned leader that they were used to? No-one noticed that the old gods had disappeared? This is ridiculous! There is not one record in Egypt or the surrounding nations to even suggest that this is what happened. To say that such incredible changes took place and no-one anywhere recorded any of it is absurd. Life in Egypt did not change, as Amenhotep III was still around to maintain order.

Before we examine the evidence of the co-regency, let's be clear about the number of years in question.

As we have seen earlier, the ONLY evidence giving Akhenaten a reign of 17 years is a wine docket. The label on an earthenware wine jar was found at Akhetaten labelled Year 17. The number 17 was crossed out and Year 1 written in its place. That is it. The entire evidence of a 17 year rule. There is no other evidence found anywhere in Egypt that suggests Akhenaten lived for much longer than 12 years. No images, records, paintings, engravings or even a fond mention by a loyal servant exist after year 12.

The argument was that as wine did not keep fresh for long at that time, and as Akhenaten was the only Pharaoh who could possibly have ruled for 17 years, then it must be him. This follows the dangerous argument of "if not him then who?" Wine jars were valuable and re-used over a number of years. One label from a wine jar from Year 17 of Amenhotep III was also found at Amarna.

If Akhenaten ruled for 17 years, why are there no records at Akhetaten after year 12 ? No paintings on the walls of tombs --- in fact, no tombs! Evidence is often frustrating. Outside the Tombs of the Nobles at Amarna, the best evidence for life at the time comes from the "Amarna Letters". These "letters" are actually clay tablets discovered at Amarna by local peasants in the 1880s. Their discovery could have been the most important find ever made of primary evidence from Amarna, but things never

Chapter 5

run that smoothly! The peasants tried to sell the tablets to visiting collectors, but no-one believed that they were genuine.

Fig 5.1   An Amarna letter.

Flinders Petrie, who was working in Egypt at the time, wrote:
A few years ago the natives, while plundering about the ruins and carrying off Akhenaten's bricks for their modern houses, hit upon the record chamber containing many hundreds of tablets. These were shown to dealers; they sent some to Dr. Oppert at Paris, who pronounced them to be forgeries, ---. At last, when they were supposed to be almost worthless, a quantity were carried about Luqsor to hawk among the dealers there and these were largely ground to pieces on the way."(1)

94

Amarna --- the missing evidence

Fortunately many were saved and they have provided a wealth of information. Written in cuneiform they are letters sent to and from Pharaoh to the rulers of Assyria, Babylonia, Mitanni and Hatte. We will be looking at more of these letters later, but the first to consider is the one known as EA 27

Fig 5.2. Amarna Letter EA27

This is a letter from Tushratta of Mitanni to Akhenaten, at the time when Akhenaten began ruling alone. This letter was sent right at the beginning of his reign. Amenhotep III is now dead but Queen Tiy lives on and is mentioned in the letter. As with most of Tushratta letters to Akhenaten, he is asking for gold and bemoaning the fact that Amenhotep III used to send lots of gold "Ask your mother Tiy --- she'll tell you!"

The important part of this letter is the hieratic docket on the left edge, beginning at the bottom of the tablet:

Year (2/12) first month of winter when one was in the Southern City.

The crucial part is broken! Is this letter sent in year 2 of Akhenaten or year 12? We will come back to the rest of the text later, but now we have our first piece of solid evidence.

Akhenaten began his sole reign *either* in (or just before) year 2 *or* year 12. There are no other choices, unless we dismiss this piece of evidence

Chapter 5

completely. Tushratta wrote frequently to Pharaoh Amenhotep III so he must have known what was going on in Egypt. The number 2 is clearly visible, so that is indisputable. We need more evidence to decide if the year was 2 or 12.

The tomb of Ramose in the Valley of the Nobles, tomb 55, shows a co-regency of longer than 2 years. Let's look at that evidence more carefully. On the South Wall of Ramose's tomb there is a scene showing a funeral procession. Four High Priests of Amun are shown in this scene – three of them simply known as "First, Second and Third Prophets of Amun." The last in the procession, the Fourth Prophet, is named as Si-Mut. Si-Mut is known from other sources as Fourth Prophet in year 20 and year 30 of Amenhotep III. He is still known as Fourth Prophet in year 34, shown at Amenhotep's second jubilee festival. Around this time, he is elevated to Second Prophet and work began on his own tomb in the Valley of the Nobles

5.3 . Wall painting showing the four prophets of Amun.

Amarna --- the missing evidence

Si-Mut was in charge of building works at Thebes at this time, and was in charge of preparing Ramose's tomb. It is clear, then, that when the Southern Wall was decorated, Si-Mut was still Fourth Prophet. He had not yet been promoted, and Amenhotep III still had many years to live. The tomb was unfinished, because Ramose moved with Akhenaten to Akhetaten in year 6 of this Pharaoh's reign. So, his tomb in the Valley of the Kings was abandoned while Si-Mut was still Fourth Prophet, no later than year 34 of Amenhotep III. This must equate to year 6 of Akhenaten.

The West Wall of Ramose's tomb was left unfinished, so it would seem that Ramose died before the work was completed. The reliefs on this wall, though, show a young Akhenaten, the early names of the Aten, Nefertiti and a Window of Appearance.

For these scenes to be inside the sealed tomb of Ramose, the conclusion must be that there was a co-regency. Amenhotep III died in Year 38/39 of his reign, so if Si-Mut is shown as Fourth Prophet on a finished wall alongside images of Pharaoh Akhenaten on an unfinished wall, the minimum co-regency must be 5 years. This assumes that Ramose was made Second Prophet immediately after finishing the Southern Wall and before he started the West Wall, and that all this took place in year 34 of Amenhotep III., so the evidence could be of a longer co-regency. But 5 years does not help us. **EA 27 gives either 2 years or 12.** We now have evidence that the co-regency was longer than 2 years. So it must read 12 years.

The Amarna letters cannot be considered as a complete set of correspondences as so many were lost, but there does appear to be a good selection that survived.

Of the 382 tablets that did survive, 350 are letters. Most of these are letters received, but a few are letters sent – or copies of letters sent. They could of course be letters that were never sent. Nothing is ever simple, though, and with just a few exceptions, the letters do not address Pharaoh by

Chapter 5

name. As the conversations are fairly mundane it is difficult to attribute them to a particular reign. Tushratta does help us, though.

Whenever Tushratta, King of Mitanni wrote to Akhenaten he made some reference to Queen Tiy. He even wrote one letter to Tiy personally. These references to Tiy are usually made to urge Akhenaten to listen to his mother, so he must have known that Akhenaten was with his mother at these times – they could not pick up the phone and speak to each other, or send emails; so they must have been together. We have already looked at EA27 and noted that it carried a docket showing that Akhenaten was in Thebes when it was written. (*the Southern City*) As this special docket was **added** to the letter, this tells us that Akhenaten was not usually resident in Thebes. Similar dockets were added to letters addressed to Amenhotep III as well, showing that some of the letters addressed to him were "forwarded" to Thebes. As we have seen, Amenhotep III and Tiy were regular visitors to Akhetaten, and because of the length of the journey must have stayed there during these visits, it is most likely that the letters were addressed to Akhenaten at Akhetaten. If we accept that there was a full co-regency of some 11/12 years, and we know that the archives office was at Akhetaten, then we can take it that letters to Amenhotep III and Akhetaten were originally sent to Akhetaten. Both kings lived at Akhetaten. Akhenaten lived their permanently and never left the city until his father's death, and Amenhotep III lived there occasionally.

There is more important evidence found in the Ghurab papyri. These papyri show that as late as year 5, Akhenaten is still known as Amenhotep IV and mention Ptah with references to other gods. Other references are made to Amenhotep III. The Ghurab papyri were written by different scribes and although they used different systems of dating, they were consistent. They appear to have been written over a period of six years, rather than sixteen years which would have been the case if there was no co-regency

Amarna --- the missing evidence

What evidence can we find in the tombs at Akhetaten? Firstly, in the Royal tomb at Amarna, scenes of grief are shown on the walls of one of the side chambers. The Royal couple's second daughter Meketaten has died. This scene is discussed in depth in chapter 8, but for now the interest lies in the fact that Amenhotep III and Queen Tiy are mentioned. Apart from Meketaten herself, everyone else mentioned in the scenes is alive – so why assume that these two are dead?

Fig 5.4 The scene of grief from the Royal tomb.

The excavations for the tombs of the Nobles at Akhetaten began as soon as the city was founded. Some scenes on the walls show just two daughters, which suggest the tombs were being decorated before the Royal Family actually moved in. Very few tombs were finished, though, and most were simply abandoned. None of these tombs show scenes of coronation or the Royal Family receiving foreign tributes. There is no evidence to show that these scenes were erased, so it must be agreed that no such scenes are shown because no such events had taken place. The building and decorating of these tombs seems to have been abandoned by year 9.

Chapter 5

Two tombs were excavated and decorated at a later date, though – the tombs of Huya and Meryre II. These two tombs provide a lot of information to prove the co-regency. Huya was The Chief Steward of Queen Tiy. Meryre II was the Overseer of the Royal Quarters. These two men would have assumed positions of real power on the death of Amenhotep III and their tombs show scenes of foreign tribute in year 12 month 2 of winter, day 8. What are these scenes celebrating? No such scenes are seen elsewhere, yet surely Pharaohs would have welcomed foreigners on many occasions throughout their reign? Yes, of course. **But the Pharaoh welcoming the foreigners before this would have been Amenhotep III.**

These celebrations with foreign dignitaries had to have had a purpose. They had not happened before, so why now? The logical reason is that they were held to celebrate the start of Akhenaten's sole rule as Pharaoh.

Also in Huya's tomb is a scene on the lintel on the north wall. This shows two royal families, back to back. One family scene shows Akhenaten, Nefertiti and their daughters whilst the other shows Amenhotep III, Tiy and Beketaten.

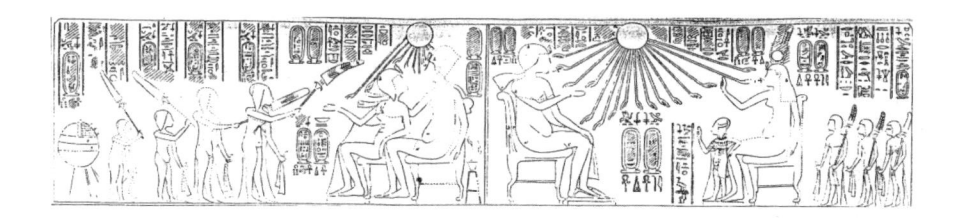

Fig 5.5. Scene from Huya's tomb showing Akhenaten and his family on the left and Amenhotep III, Tiy and Beketaten on the right.

Amarna --- the missing evidence

Fig5.6 . Scenes of Foreign Tribute from the tomb of Huya

Fig 5.7. Scene of Foreign Tribute. Tomb of Meryre II

Chapter 5

The inscription from the lintel reads on the North Wall of Huya's tomb reads: *Long live the father – god and king – the living Ra, ruler of the two horizons, rejoicing on the horizon in the name of the Brilliance which comes from the Aten, who gives life for ever and ever, the king of south and north etc. Neferkheperure Waenre, who gives life; the King of South and North, lord of the Two Lands, Neb-maat-re, and the great Queen and Queen Mother Tiy who lives for ever and ever.*

This scene has been the subject of many debates, with some arguing that as the new religion of the Aten does not have the same references to the dead, that Amenhotep III was not actually alive when the scene was painted. This creates far more problems than it solves, though. If Amenhotep III was dead when the scene was painted, and there are no references to him as being dead, then how can we trust any of the images that we are shown in any of the scenes? If we follow this logically, looking at the scene in the royal tomb, showing mourning at the death of Meketaten, how can we be sure that Akhenaten or Nefertiti were alive? How can we be sure that Akhenaten and Nefertiti were alive when Huya and the other nobles received their golden collars?

Logically, the figures in all of the scenes in all of the tombs were alive when they were painted, otherwise everything we see must be doubted.

This scene also finalises the argument over the parentage of Beketaten. Her title is given as:

The King's daughter of his body, beloved by him.

The king in the scene is *Amenhotep III.*

Another interesting piece of evidence is a limestone block from Athribis which bears the cartouches of Amenhotep IV and Amenhotep III in this order and ***facing the same way***.

Amarna --- the missing evidence

The cartouches are shown below:

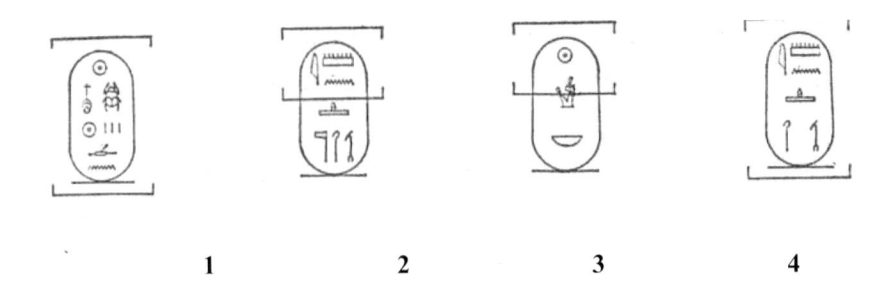

      1   2   3   4

Fig 5.8 Akhenaten's cartouches nos 1 and 2, followed by Amenhotep III's cartouches 3 and 4

As this shows the name of Amenhotep IV before his name change, the block cannot be dated later than year 5, and if Amenhotep III was dead and being honoured by his son, they would be ***facing each other***. The only conclusion can be that the two kings are alive together.

An avid opponent of the co-regency theory, Donald Redford is happy to admit that these two Kings were alive together:

"Amenhotep III reigned for about 40 years and then abdicated (under pressure?) in favour of his son Akhenaten. The latter reigned for 21 years, during the first nine of which his father was ending his days in retirement" (2)

There is no evidence of any Pharaoh "abdicating". Pharaoh was the direct link to God. If Amenhotep III had lived on for a further nine years after his year 39, there would have been records, and he would have been about 61 years old when he died. All reference to Amenhotep III ends at year 39, so the 9 years mentioned above must start at year 30.

In 1962 Professor Kenneth Kitchen published an extensive study into the Amarna Pharaohs and the rulers of the surrounding nations. (3) In

Chapter 5

particular, he concentrated on Suppiluliuma, ruler of the Hittites, and concluded that there was most probably a co-regency between Amenhotep III and Akhenaten of between 8 and 11 years. Professor Kitchen also looked at Tushratta, king of Mitanni, who played such an important part in the lives of Amenhotep III and Akhenaten. He writes:

"As Tushratta was murdered a year after Tutankhamen's he reigned at least 20 years as a contemporary of Amenhotep III plus 8 years of Akhenaten's sole rule, 8 years of Tutankhamen and one of Aye, a total of 37 years and would be 53 or 55 years old at death if he acceded aged about 16 or 18."

As nothing is heard of Akhenaten after year 12, it would shorten Tushratta's rule by 5 years, giving 3 years Akhenaten's sole rule in Professor Kitchen's calculations. If Akhenaten had a sole rule of 17 years, Tushratta would have ruled for 46 years and died age 64. As he was murdered by his son, who was only about 20 years old, his age at death would be very high. Suppiluliuma's three known campaigns would have extended over a much longer period of time than would seem reasonable.

One things is certain. The Foreign dignitaries brought the plague to Akhetaten. In the plague prayers of Mursilli, one of Suppiluliuma's successors, it is recorded that after invading Egypt his soldiers took captives.

"But when they brought back to the Hatti land, the prisoners which they had taken, a plague broke out among the prisoners and these began to die. When they moved the prisoners to the Hatti land, these prisoners carried the plague into the Hatti land. From that day on people have been dying in the Hatti land."

The text tells us what we already knew - that a great plague was ravaging the Middle East at the time. The same plague is mentioned in the Amarna Letters EA 11, EA 35, EA 96 and EA 932. Amenhotep III built the Malkata Palace in *"a place which had not been used in historic times."*

Amarna --- the missing evidence

Away from any plague. Akhenaten built his new city of Akhetaten in *"a place which had not been used in historic times."*

Apart from the scenes of mourning in rooms alpha and gamma in the Royal Tomb, nothing else is known of life at Akhetaten after the ceremony attended by foreign dignitaries. There are no further decorations to tombs, no more scenes of worship to the Aten – nothing. Everything comes to an end in year 12.

Notes

1 Giles, FJ.,1997 *The Amarna Age: Western Asia.* Oxford. Aris & Phillips Ltd

2 Redford, D.,1959. Some observations on Amarna Chronology. *Journal of Egyptian Archaeology* edition 45

3 Kitchen, K., 1962 . *Suppiluliuma and the Amarna Pharaohs.* Liverpool. Liverpool Press.

Chapter 5

To conclude:

Version 1 (the Established version)

Akhenaten succeeded his father as Pharaoh of Egypt.
He ruled for 17 years (evidence of the wine jar)
Akhenaten moved the capital city of Egypt from Thebes to Akhetaten.

Version 2 (My version)

Akhenaton's rule was conducted alongside his father.
The Amarna letters provide evidence of this co-regency:
EA27 states "Year 12"
The correspondences from Mitanni prove a co-regency.
The coronation scenes is shown as year 12 in the tombs of Huya and Meryre II
Si-Mut became Second Prophet after Akhenaten had become co-regent.

You decide.

Chapter 6

Years 3, 6, 9 and 12

"Any man whose errors take ten years to correct is quite a man."

--- **J. Robert Oppenheimer**

There are four years in the life of Akhenaten that are vital to our understanding of his reign. Interestingly, these have three years between each one.

Akhenaten built temples to the Aten at Karnak in the early years of his life, and it must have been around **year 3** that the idea of moving was first considered.

We have already seen that **year 6** was the date of the founding of Akhetaten. In Year 6 his adventure began. He was building a new city, and eventually he would be on his own. He would have his own city, his own "Nobles", his own family and his own God. Life was to be wonderful – and for a while it probably was.

It took two years or more to build this new city. Two years of enthusiasm and expectation. We have already seen that from **year 6** Akhenaten was quite happy to live in a tent. Anyone who has ever been camping with children must know how difficult it is with children, but not only did Nefertiti accompany her husband and bring the children with her, she almost certainly gave birth to her fourth child Neferneferuaten-ta-sherit whilst camping out waiting for the Palace to be built.

To understand the sequence of events, it is necessary to examine the chronology of the construction of the tombs of the Nobles at Akhetaten. As

Amarna --- the missing evidence

we have seen, 25 private tombs have been discovered at the site of Akhetaten. The Royal Tomb has also been uncovered and its findings very well recorded.

The tombs at Akhetaten are not unlike most of the 18th Dynasty tombs on the West Bank at Thebes but the designs of the tombs are more varied. The tombs appear to have been mass produced in the space of a few years but no two are exactly alike in design and decoration. Most of the private tombs usually consist of a court, surrounded on three sides by a wall, cut from the rock in the cliffs behind the city. A second chamber or hall lies behind the court and a shaft or stairway opens into the floor leading down to the actual burial chamber.

As you have seen, six of the 25 tombs are known as the North Tombs and the other 19 form the Southern Tombs. Of the six northern tombs, two sit apart from the others – the tombs of Huya and Meryre II.

The numbering of the tombs is deceptive. They were not numbered in this way when they were built, and a quick look at the map shows that these two tombs were an afterthought. Where should they be built? Where was there space? Although the decoration of the walls in the tombs of the Nobles varied, they all followed a similar theme, and this was a big change from the decoration on the walls of the tombs at Thebes. Scenes in the 18th Dynasty Tombs at Thebes show the lives of the owners.

They show how brave they were or how good they were, and boast of the qualities that will provide entry to the afterlife. The scenes in the tombs built at Akhetaten are always related to Akhenaten and his family. The scenes feature Akhenaten together with the royal family making offerings before heaped altars under the rays of the god Aten. In no less than seven tombs, the royal family is depicted at a table, or drinking wine together.

Chapter 6

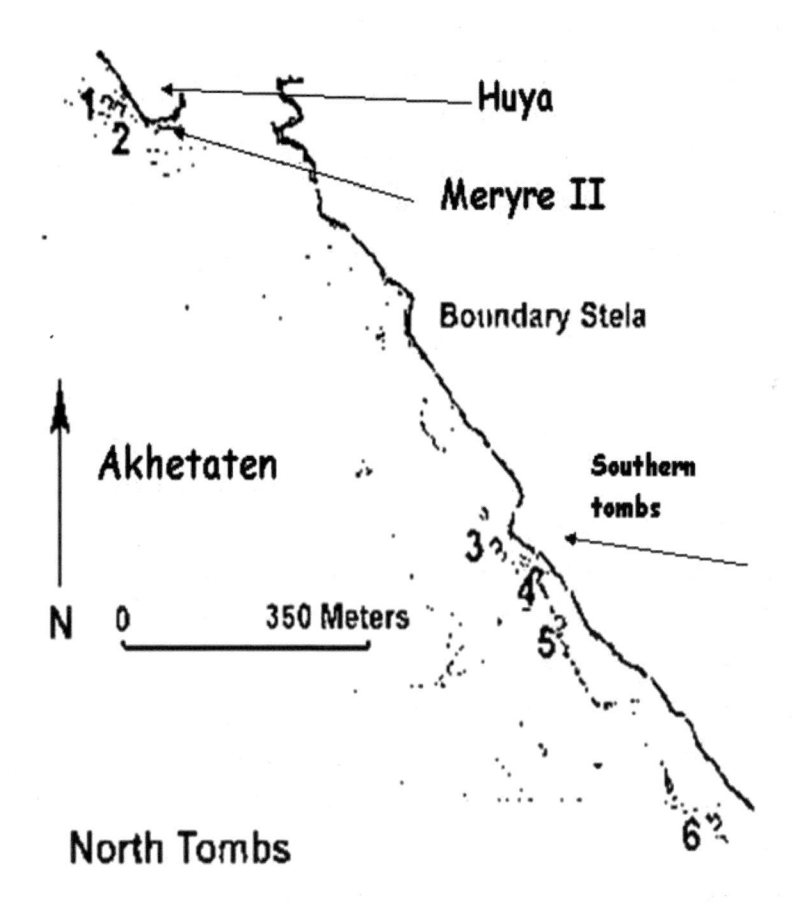

Fig 6.1 Map of the Tombs.

The tomb owners are often shown receiving rewards from Akhenaten or Nefertiti and texts tell how wonderful this is. No expense seems to have been spared in their cutting and decoration. The rock is a very poor limestone, though, and the tombs had to be heavily plastered before being decorated. Decorations on plaster did not have enduring properties, as the plaster was liable to shrink.

Amarna --- the missing evidence

So, mass produced tombs with similar decoration throughout. It is most likely that these tombs were gifts from Akhenaten to his Nobles, and that he had the greatest say in what went on the walls. They were excavated early in the life of the City, probably in the first flush of enthusiasm.

Now we come to the interesting part. As we have seen, few of the tombs were ever finished, and apart from Tomb 1 (Huya) and tomb 2 (Meryre II), work on the tombs appears to have stopped round about Year 9. There are no scenes in the tombs which show events later than **year 9**. Work stopped in **year 9**.

But what happened to the Nobles? There is only evidence of two of the tombs ever being used for a burial, so we might expect the Nobles to be quite upset over this. Yet there is no evidence of a rebellion amongst these men. Did they not fear for their immortal souls? If not, why not? They did not fear for their immortal souls because they knew that their final resting place was to be back in Thebes where their hearts would be weighed by Anubis, and Osiris would grant them a life in the after-world. The Nobles were clearly not taken up with the new god Aten. Yet we have been taught that Akhenaten "expunged" all of the old gods.

It is quite likely that the nobles left the city soon after **year 9**. In the scene above the lintel in Huya's tomb, a very worn, ageing Amenhotep III shown taking tea with his family. His reign was clearly nearing its end and a new Pharaoh would soon take his place. The nobles would have realised that Akhenaten could not have ruled alone. This could have created an opportunity for these "caretaker" nobles to start thinking of a return to Thebes.

It is often said that no other gods were worshiped at Akhetaten, but is this case? In the 1920s, Thomas Peet and Leonard Woolley found part of a painted prayer to Amun in a private chapel in the Workmen's Village at Amarna. They also found a small limestone stelae dedicated to Isis. In her

Chapter 6

book, Anna Stevens (1) found that the ordinary people living at Akhetaten still held on to their old religion. There is evidence that they simply humoured Akhenaten and his new religion of the Aten – they had not turned from their old gods, and had no intention of doing so. They had moved with Akhenaten to a new life in the desert, but not because they followed his new god. We have no reason to believe that the nobles had any greater belief in this new god either.

Back to the tombs of the nobles then. What was going on? Akhenaten must have been aware that work had stopped on the tombs of his nobles surely? Was he unable to visit the cliffs to observe progress? Was he running out of workmen? We can only guess, but the image of bubbling life in this new, glorious city is gradually being eroded.

Akhetaten was a chimera. A grotesque product of the imagination – Akhenaten's imagination. His father arranged for his protection there, and kept an eye on his son. Akhenaten worshiped the Aten, but did anyone else really share his views?

What else happened in or by year 9?

By **year 9** Akhenaten and Nefertiti had fathered four daughters:

- Merytaten ('Beloved of the Aten')
- Meketaten ('Protected by the Aten')
- Ankhesenpaaten ('Living through the god Aten')
- Neferneferuaten ta-Sherit ('Exquisite beauty of the sun disc')

It is interesting to note that these four daughters had names configured with the Aten, Two more daughters appear to have been born to the Royal couple after **year 9**, Neferneferure ('Exquisite beauty of **Re**') and Setepenre

Amarna --- the missing evidence

('Chosen of **Re**') There is no mention of the Aten in their names. Just the ancient sun god Re. Around **year 9** the Chief Sculptor Bek was replaced by Tuthmose, and the art form changed to create a softer image of the family. (see chapter 4)   The name of the Aten, as written in Cartouches also changed.

At the start of his reign, the Aten's name is written in two cartouches corresponding to the two cartouches of Akhenaten ,and are followed by the words "given life for ever and ever". These words were usually applied to Pharaoh, and had never before been applied to a god's name. It seems a strange epithet as if the Aten is the supreme God, who has the power to give him "life for ever and ever?" The later form of the Aten name begins "**Re** Lives" with "Ruler of the Horizon"

The Early Names   The Later Names

Fig 6.2.   The Aten names

Chapter 6

The later form of the Aten name begins "**Re** Lives" with "Ruler of the Horizon".

(a) Full Earlier Titulary and Name of the Aten.

(b) Later Form of the Aten's Name.

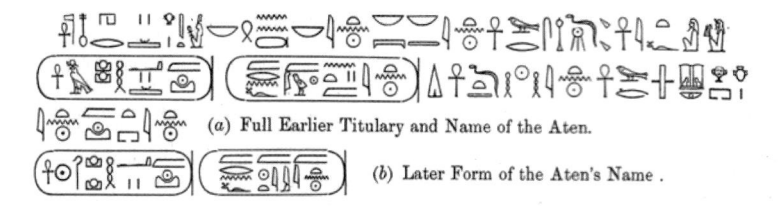

Fig 6.3. The Aten Names

According to Battiscombe Gunn in his "Notes on the Aten and his name":

"The change from the earlier to the later cartouche name of the Aten took place at the latest in the 9th year and not earlier than the middle of the 8th year." (2)

It has often been considered that the "Amarna Period" covered a number of years with Akhenaten in charge. There does now appear to be two separate "seasons" with **Re** becoming more dominant in the last few years of Akhenaten's life.

So, back to the question; ***What happened in year 9?*** From wine jar dockets and artefacts found on the site of the new city, it is clear, though, that Amenhotep III and Queen Tiy visited their son from time to time. These visits became more frequent after **year 9.**

It was around **year 9** that work started on the tombs of Huya and Meryre II. The titles of these two Nobles gives us the clue. **Huya** was *"Chief Steward of Queen Tiy"*. Queen Tiy must have been concerned. Her husband Amenhotep III was showing signs of age and it was obvious to Tiy that one

Amarna --- the missing evidence

day her son Akhenaten would be ruling Egypt alone. Her influence after **year 9** seems to have been aimed at "softening" her son's extreme views.

Tiy now appears in scenes in Huya's tomb, sometimes alone.

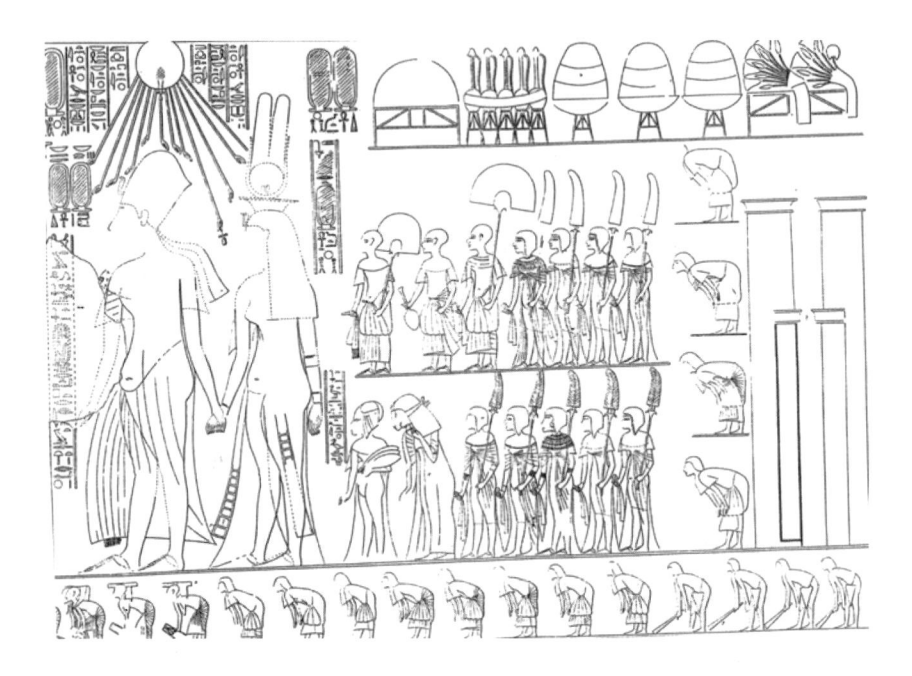

Fig 6.4. Akhenaten leading his mother, Queen Tiy from Huya's tomb.

The Egypt Exploration Society's expedition of 1931 excavated a small chapel. John Pendlebury was in charge and he reported finding some pieces of a pink granite bowl. It bore the inscriptions of the *later* Aten names together with "Neb-maat-re) and followed by "in Akhetaten" (3) The names of the Aten did not change until year 9, so we must accept that Amenhotep III was still alive after year 9. There does not appear to be ant sensible reason why Akhenaten should write his father's names beside the Aten names ten years after the latter's death.

Chapter 6

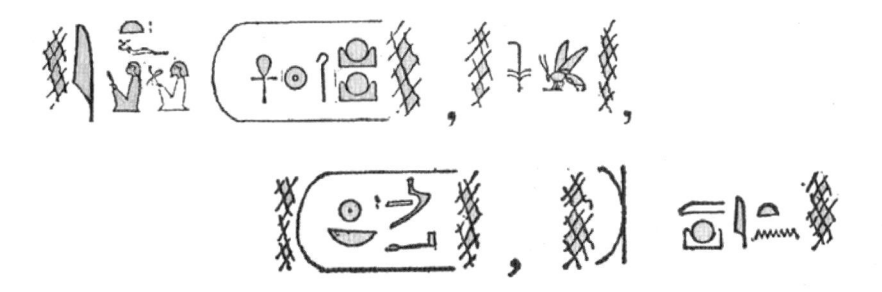

Fig 6.5 The late Aten names and Amenhotep III

Meryre II's title was "Overseer of the Royal Quarters", but his many titles included that of *"Superintendent of the Harem of Nefertiti."* **The owners of the two later tombs both rise to prominence after year 9.** Nefertiti's title changes at the same time from *Royal Wife* to .Great Royal Wife. Tiy and Nefertiti are clearly ladies of influence after Year 9.
There are no further scenes of life at Akhetaten after year 9 except in the tombs of Huya and Meryre II, and in the Royal Tomb.

The scenes on the walls of the tombs of these two Nobles relate to Years 9 to 12 of Akhenaten's reign, presumably reflecting the time it took to carve out the tombs and plaster the walls. Scenes show the royal family with all six daughters, and the royal family entertaining Amenhotep III and Tiy. Much has been written about these scenes with some authors claiming them to be images of Amenhotep III and Tiy after they have died. Yet we know from the Amarna letters that Tiy was alive in Akhenaten's **year 12**, so why would she be shown in a scene with her dead husband?

The earliest this scene could have been painted would be year 10 and as Tiy is seen on her own with her son and his family after this, it would

Amarna --- the missing evidence

seem most likely that Amenhotep III died after year 10 – probably late in year 11 of Akhenaten's reign.

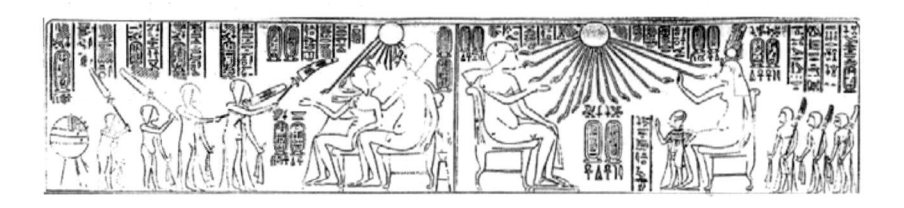

Fig 6.6. Scene showing Amenhotep III from Huya's tomb.

In the Amarna letter EA26, Tushratta writes to Tiy:

To Tiy, Lady of Egypt. Thus speaks Tushratta, King of Mitanni Everything is well with me. May everything be well with you. May everything go well for your house, your son, may everything be perfectly well for your soldiers and for everything belonging to you.

You are the one who knows that I have always felt friendship for Mimmuriya your husband, and that Mimmuriya, your husband, on his part always felt friendship for me. And the things that I wrote and told Mimmuriya, your husband, and the things that Mimmuriya, your husband, on his part wrote and told me incessantly, were known to you, Keliya and Mane. But it is you who knows better than anybody, the things we have told each other. No one knows them better.

You should continue sending joyful embassies, one after another. Do not suppress them. I shall not forget the friendship with Mimmuriya, your husband. At this moment and more than ever, I have ten times more friendship for your son, Napkhuria.

You are the one who knows the words of Mimmuriya, your husband, but you have not sent me yet the gift of homage which Mimmuriya, your husband, has ordered to be sent to me. I have asked Mimmuriya, your

Chapter 6

husband, for massive gold statues. But your son has gold-plated statues of wood. As the gold is like dust in the country of your son, why have they been the reason for such pain, that your son should not have given them to me? Neither has he given me what his father had been accustomed to give.

Amenhotep III is clearly dead. Akhenaten is clearly the sole ruler of Egypt --- but Tiy is clearly in charge!

Tiy appears in many of scenes in the tombs with her daughter Beketaten, Akhenaten's younger sister. As Amenhotep III would have been Beketaten's father this shows how deeply influenced he was by the Aten. So, we now have a situation at Akhetaten where Amenhotep III and Queen Tiy visit regularly, and when Amenhotep III eventually dies, Queen Tiy moves to the city to join her son.

The last scenes in the tombs of Huya and Meryre II date to *year 12*. These scenes will be discussed in detail later, but for now it is important to understand this dating.

After year 12 there is nothing.

Nothing at all is recorded of life in Akhenaten's city. It all comes to a stop. Apart from scenes on the walls of the Royal Tomb showing the grief of the royal family at the death of their second daughter Meketaten, there is no record of any other death in the city.

The scenes in the tombs of Huya and Meryre II show a festival where Akhenaten receives tributes from foreign dignitaries. This is the only time foreign dignitaries visited Akhetaten and it brought both celebration and disaster to the city. We can read the *Plague Prayers* of the Hittite king Mursilli, king of the Hittites:

'When the Egyptians became frightened, they asked outright for one of his [Suppiluliuma's] sons to take over the kingship. But when my father gave them one of his sons, they led him there and they killed him. My father let his anger run away with him, he went to war against Egypt and attacked Egypt.

Amarna --- the missing evidence

He smote the foot soldiers and the charioteers of the country of Egypt. But when they brought back to the Hatti land, the prisoners which they had taken, a plague broke out among the prisoners and these began to die. When they moved the prisoners to the Hatti land, these prisoners carried the plague into the Hatti land. From that day on people have been dying in the Hatti land.'

Fig 6.7. (above and next page) Akhenaten and Nefertiti entertain Queen Tiy and Beketaten.

We know that there was a plague in Egypt and the Middle East at the time. The same plague is mentioned in the Amarna Letters EA 11, EA 35, EA 96 and EA 932. Amenhotep III seems to have moved from Memphis to an area outside Thebes city centre to avoid the plague, and Akhenaten built Akhetaten as a safe haven. The visit of the Foreigners was the first time this latter safe haven was breached. Given the scale of this epidemic, it is likely

Chapter 6

Notes:

1. Stevens ,A., 2006 Private Religion at Amarna. Oxford : Archaeopress

1903-1908: Norman de Garis Davies published the tombs of Amarna in six volumes.

2. Gunn, B., 1923. Notes on the Aten and his names. *Journal of Egyptian Archaeology*

3 Giles, F J., 1970 Ikhnaton Legend and History. London. Hutchinson.

Amarna --- the missing evidence

To conclude:

Version 1 (The established version)

Akhenaten lived in his new city for 11 years.

Scenes of life during those 11 years appear on the walls of the tombs of the nobles.

Meketaten, the second daughter of the Royal couple, died in childbirth.

Her son was Tutankhamen.

Version 2 (My version)

Akhenaten lived in his new city for about 6 years.

Scenes of life during the first 3 years appear on the walls of the tombs of the nobles.

Meketaten died of the plague soon after the great festival in year 12,

Akhenaten died around year 12 following the great festival in year 12.

Tutankhamen was Akhenaten's younger brother.

You decide

𓆑𓊪𓏤𓏤𓏤

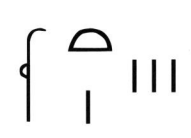

Pause for thought

Pause for thought.

"There are pauses amidst study, and even pauses of seeming idleness, in which a process goes on which may be likened to the digestion of food. In those seasons of repose, the powers are gathering their strength for new efforts; as land which lies fallow recovers itself for tillage". ---

J. W. Alexander

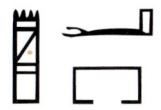

Before we move on to see what new evidence is available to help us understand this troubled period of history, let's stop for a moment and review the evidence so far.

Looking at things logically, we cannot really believe that Akhenaten ever ruled Egypt independently. To have ruled this great nation successfully from the remote desert regions, with untrained "nobles" and a total devotion to his family and the Aten makes the idea of an independent rule quite unacceptable. Is this really the image a King should present? The ages of our characters just does not fit the accepted version of events.. Take Aye, the future Pharaoh. However we interpret his earlier title of "God's Father", the use of the word "father" tells us that he was certainly a good bit older than Akhenaten. If Akhenaten was born in year 20 of his father, Amenhotep III's reign, and ruled for 17 years independently after the latter's death, the Aye was probably born in year 1 of Amenhotep III and would be 56/57 years old at Akhenaten's death.

Amarna --- the missing evidence

The ruler of one of the greatest countries in the world?

Pause for thought

Add 3 years for Smenkhkare and 10 for Tutankhamen, then Aye would have been 70 when he took the throne! Whilst a possibility it must be unlikely. Especially as we are told he later married Tutankhamen's young widow.

If, however, Akhenaten was born in year 8 of his father's reign. Aye was most likely about 20 years old. Amenhotep III and Akhenaten were both dead thirty years later, and the Pharaoh who shared the second co-regency at the end of Akhenaten's did not outlive him by more than a year. Aye would then have been about 61 when he took the throne. Much more likely considering life expectancy at the time.

The religion of the country did not change during Akhenaten's time at Akhetaten. There are no records of any changes or unrest at any time in the late 18th dynasty. Amun ruled supreme at Thebes.

Akhenaten was not physically deformed. He probably had an elongated skull but the rest was part of his religion – a part that we will probably never understand.

Taking a holistic view of this period of history, these are by far the most reasonable conclusions. But what happened when Amenhotep III finally dies? Does Egypt really allow Akhenaten to rule alone?

Let's take a look now at the events after the death of Akhenaten's father.

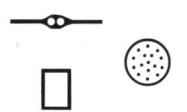

Chapter 7

Smenkhkare

"Discovery consists of seeing what everybody has seen and thinking what nobody has thought." --- **Albert Szent-Gyorgyi**

"**Excepting a ring found at Gurob, this king is solely known from his remains at Tell el Amarna** " --- (1)

More than a hundred years later, this would still holds true, but as you can see in fig 7.1 below, the name on the ring at Gurob does **not** say *Smenkhkare*. The understandable mistake was made because of a long standing confusion over this Pharaoh's *nomen* and *prenomen*. (2)

Fig 7.1 Gurob Ring

This is the ring Petrie referred to in his quotation. This does not say Smenkhkare, but rather the **prenomen** of the new **Pharaoh Ankhkheperure**.

Amarna --- the missing evidence

Smenkhkare was the most mysterious figure to come out of the Amarna period. He apparently reigned for about three years, and spent some length of time as Akhenaten's coregent. The evidence concerning Smenkhkare is sparse and patchy, and theories about Smenkhkare are built on very unstable foundations. In this chapter, you can judge for yourself by examining some exclusive new evidence.

Nothing is known of Smenkhkare's life. Egyptologists can only guess who his parents might have been, where he lived and where he died. In the absence of a better candidate it has been assumed that his body was the one found by --- in Kv55.

Comments like this are typical of the statements made about Smenkhkare. There is no substance to the statements. None of the Amarna letters were addressed to Smenkhkare, yet one or two appear to have been addressed to his "successor," Tutankhamen.

Let us for a moment recap on what we have uncovered so far. We now know that Akhenaten moved his family to a new City of the Aten, whilst his father, Amenhotep III ruled on in Thebes. There is no evidence anywhere in Egypt of any protests over a change in religion at this time and quite clearly if the religion of a country like Egypt had changed so dramatically it would have been recorded. Akhetaten was built as a city for the Aten, where Akhenaten and his growing family lived with a retinue of loyal followers, selected by Akhenaten and his father to ensure everything ran smoothly. (Chapter 3)

Amenhotep III eventually dies, and Akhenaten rules alone. But does he? There is plenty of evidence of a co-regency at the end of Akhenaten's reign, but who was his co-regent?

There is still no record of any concerns over a change in religion, yet

Chapter 7

we are told that Akhenaten turned against the god Amun. Akhenaten lives on in his new city, so what is going on in Thebes? The administrative capital remained at Thebes. Who is there in charge? If we accept that the religion of Egypt did not change, then someone must have been keeping things running smoothly in Thebes.

So let us see what we actually know of Smenkhkare. There are only two occasions where the actual nomen "SMENKHKARE" is supposedly recorded. The name in full is supposed to be

"SMENKHKARE DJESER KHEPER U RE"

It is worth noting that DJESER KHEPER U RE was actually part of Horemheb's name, the last Pharaoh of the 18th dynasty, and it must be considered highly unlikely that he would adopt the name used by any Pharaoh of the Amarna period! These cartouches were only supposed to have been seen in one place on one wall at Amarna. They did not appear anywhere else in Egypt.

So who claims to have seen the cartouches of a Pharaoh Smenkhkare? Well, actually, no-one!

The discovery of a set of cartouches was made on the North wall of the tomb of Meryre II, by the British explorer Robert Hay about 1830. Robert Hay was a Scotsman who arrived in Egypt in 1824, aged 25, having recently inherited the family estate back home. He was an artist and explorer, not an Egyptologist, but his work was meticulous and the copies he made were as good as could be expected at the time. His work clearly shows the damage to the cartouches caused by damp and decay, and he ***does not*** claim to see the name Smenkhkare.

Amarna --- the missing evidence

Two French explorers, Nestor L'Hote and Prisse D'Avenes recorded the cartouches in 1839 and 1843 respectively. Hippolyte Antoine l'Hôte (Nestor) (1804 – 1842) was a French artist and explorer. He published hundreds of sketches and drawings of Egypt and its monuments. Achille-Constant-Théodore-Émile Prisse d'Avennes (1807 –1879) was a French artist. The fourth and last person to see these vital inscriptions was Karl Richard Lepsius (pictured left) in 1845. In Lepsius we have one of the first of the modern Egyptologists, with an understanding of Hieroglyphs. His work was extensive throughout Egypt, and particularly important because it described many sites that have deteriorated today, including Meryre II's tomb at Amarna. Many inscriptions, tombs scenes and other material that would be lost to us today if Lepsius had not carried out his timely explorations, and it is to Lepsius that we turn to understand what was recorded on this wall.

So, we have an early explorer and Artist (Robert Hay) followed ten years later by two more artists. Only Lepsius can claim any real credibility as an Egyptologist, with an early understanding of Hieroglyphs. These cartouches were recorded over 150 years ago. Anyone who has been inside the Tombs of the Nobles will appreciate how dark they are. These cartouches are on the North Wall of Meryre II's tomb, well away from the small amount of daylight penetrating the entrance. To be able to record anything is a great achievement; to record accurately by anyone without an understanding of hieroglyphs is almost impossible.

If the late Bill Murnane had been the first to see these cartouches, or Barry Kemp who is currently in charge of the site at Amarna, then the results would have been much more certain. With their wealth of experience and modern arc lights we would be left in no doubt what had been carved there. When Petrie examined the tomb during his 1891-92 expedition, the cartouches had gone.

Chapter 7

"This inscription in the tomb is now totally destroyed, in the smashings made a few years ago: so that it can never be studied."

The four explorers recorded their findings in different ways. Robert Hay did not write up his findings. He simply kept his original sketch books and notes which are now to be found in the British Library. Prisse D'Avennes and Nestor L'Hote's works were published in 1847 (Nestor L'Hote's work was published after his death.) Karl Richard Lepsius published his work on his return from Egypt in 1845. These dates are important, as you will see later.

For fifty years this Pharaoh was known as S aA Khkare.

Our next explorer is a man held in the highest regard today. William Matthew Flinders Petrie (known to everyone as "Flinders") began his long career as an archaeologist when he was a young man. Petrie's father was a surveyor who taught his son how to use the most modern surveying equipment of the time. This early training instilled in the young Petrie a respect for measurement and accuracy which would inform and influence his life's work in archaeology. In 1892, Petrie became the first Edwards Professor of Egyptian Archaeology and Philology at University College, London. This chair had been funded by Amelia Edwards who was a keen supporter and admirer of Petrie.

Petrie was a pioneer in the field of Egyptian archaeology, with his careful and scientific excavation techniques. His emphasis on recording the physical dispersal of objects in a site rather than simply digging for objects made his excavation techniques unique for his time. Petrie trained many of the best archaeologists of the day who worked side-by-side with him, learning his techniques.

Flinders Petrie, in his excavations at Amarna discovered hundreds of

Amarna --- the missing evidence

ring bezels. Many bore the name Ankh Kheper u re, the *prenomen* of this successor to Akhenaten, and two bear the name Smenkhkare Djeser Kheper u re, although each has a different layout to the hieroglyphs. Just two. (3)

These two are Petrie's names Smenkhkare

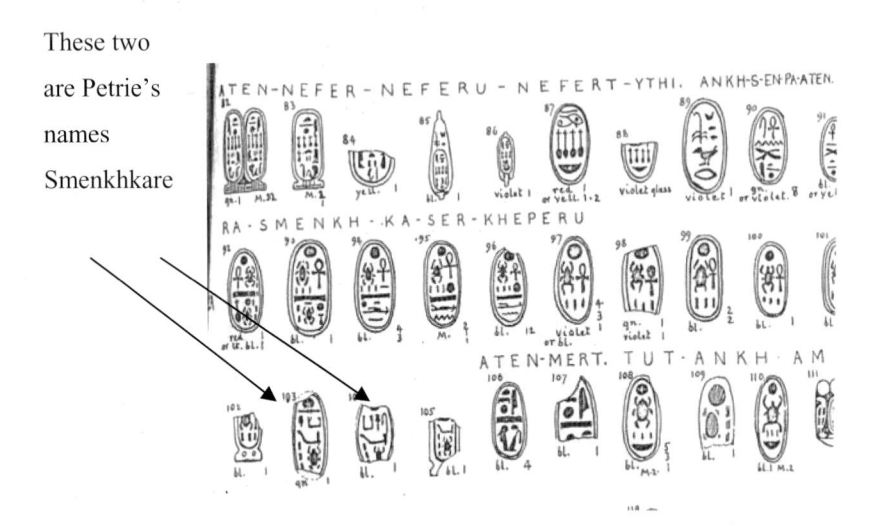

Fig 7.2 Petrie's Rings.

Petrie could not refer to the original cartouches as they had gone, so he turned to the work of Prisse D'Avennes and Karl Lepsius to compare the writing on his ring bezels. He later wrote:

Lepsius read it as Ra se hek ka ser kheperu (L.D.iii.99 a); Prisse as Ra se ka nekht kheperu, but he shows that it was injured in his time (Pr M p3); unhappily it has all been destroyed in the horrible mutilation which has recently befallen the tombs here. (4)

There is not much logic here as Lepsius entered the tomb after Prisse, so if the damage had been done before Prisse's visit, it could not have been restored for Lepsius. It was Petrie who decided that his two rings must refer to a Pharaoh, and "Smenkhkare" was created. This is a great leap, from

Chapter 7

two ring bezels reading Smenkhkare to a Pharaoh of Egypt. Petrie found hundreds of ring bezels at Amarna, and two of these bear the name Smenkhkare Djeser Kheper u re, although each has a different layout to the hieroglyphs. These are simply names on rings, though, and if all of the ring bezels found by Petrie referred to Pharaohs or their wives, then we are missing a great number of Kings! It will help if we understand where these rings were found.

Among the rings are dozens bearing the name Ankh-kheper-u-re, all found, according to Petrie *"in the rubbish mounds of the Palace"* (5)

Fig 7.3 . Ankheperure rings from Amarna. (6)

The two Smenkhkare ring bezels :*" were found in the town"*

These were the two rings found that bear the names Smenkhkare Djeser kheper u re written in two different ways. Hardly where you would expect to find the King's rings! *In the town.* Why were Akhenaten's ring bezels, those of his daughters, Nefertiti and Ankh-kheper-u-re found at the Palace site, but not the rare two with the name Smenkhkare? Without the works of Lepsius and Prisse, Petrie would simply have added these ring bezels to his collection of those belonging to unknown residents of the city. Which is where they belong. There is nothing to suggest that these rings belonged to a member of the Royal family, let alone a Pharaoh.

Between 1902 and 1907 Norman de Garis Davies, working under the guidance of the Egypt Exploration Fund (now Society), conducted a

Amarna --- the missing evidence

comprehensive survey of the tombs of Akhenaten's nobles, in the cliffs at Amarna. During this time Davies worked at El-Amarna for between six to eight weeks a year, usually in the winter, but sometimes in the heat of summer, during which time he succeeded in copying the decorated and inscribed tombs and the Boundary Stelae.

He published his findings in six volumes "The Rock Tombs of Tel Amarna" As the cartouches in Meryre II's tomb had disappeared, Davies published Lepsius' versions of the names of the Pharaoh. He did not use any of the other three versions, just Lepsius'.

By now, Flinders Petrie has changed the Pharaoh's name from S aA Khkare. to S men khka re and as Petrie and Davies knew each other well, the new name stuck. Another well respected Egyptologist now enters the scene. Percy Newberry who had worked extensively in Egypt and later wrote many articles for the Egypt Exploration Fund (now the Egypt Exploration Society) Newberry had examined the tombs of the nobles, but he arrived after the important cartouches had been destroyed. Copies of the four sets of cartouches were published by Percy Newberry in 1928. (7) This is where the problems start.

Percy Newberry joined the controversy. In his article, Newberry writes that he is convinced that the reading should be Smenkhkare Djeser Kheper u re and backed up his argument by referring to ring bezels found by Petrie during his 1891-92 searches at Amarna.

Newberry printed copies of the cartouches as drawn by our four explorers. Before we examine the centre cartouche, the ***prenomen***, in greater detail, let's see what the four explorers saw. They are all 100% certain that the ***prenomen***, the name given to Pharaoh on his accession to the throne is definitely "Ankh-kheper-u-re".

Chapter 7

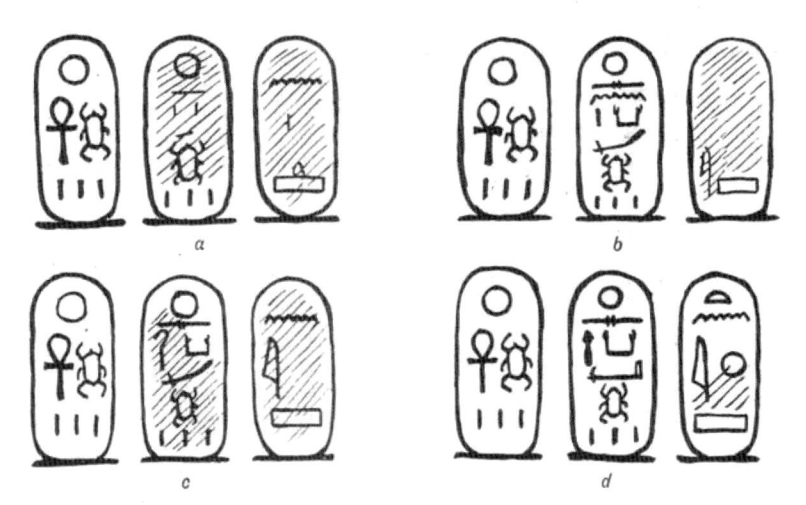

Fig 7.4 Newberry's cartouches.

(a) is reported to be the work of Robert Hay. (b) Is that of Nestor L'Hote.

(c) Prisse D'Avennes.   (d) Karl Richard Lepsius.

We must remember that these cartouches had been carved over the top of Akhenaten's names, and as the only alteration needed here was to change his "nfr" sign into an "Ankh" sign, this was probably the easiest and clearest alteration to make.

So, this Pharaoh was definitely

Lord of the Two Lands Ankh-Kheper-u-Re

Amarna --- the missing evidence

Who was his wife? Her name should be in the last cartouche.

According to Newberry,

Merytaten?

Only Lepsius published this as Merytaten. "Meryt – Aten".

Robert Hay apparently saw a Htp sign and an "n" at the top, but little else. Prisse D'Avennes and Nestor L'Hote see different hieroglyphs. Our first three explorers all record the third cartouches as being very badly damaged as indicated by the grey lines running through.

So, what was his *nomen*? His birth name? His "Son of Re" name? This is where the problems start. The *nomen* has been recorded for about 100 years as "S-men-khka-re" yet this is not a *nomen* – it is a *prenomen*. A throne name. For the centre cartouche to read Smenkhkare, we have a Pharaoh with no *nomen*, but two *prenomens*. Not really very likely! For the centre cartouche:

a) Robert Hay. Newberry dismisses as "quite indefinite".
b) Nestor L'Hote. Newberry says "blundered badly"
c) Prisse D'avennes. Newberry says that Prisse saw the sign HqA not
d) Karl Richard Lepsius. Lepsius saw a A not

According to Percy Newberry NONE of the explorers saw the same cartouches, and this does seem unlikely. **NONE of the explorers saw**

Chapter 7

SMENKHKARE.

So let's sum up what we have discovered so far : The name Smenkhkare was NOT recorded in the cartouches on the wall of Meryre II's tomb. None of the early explorers saw the name Smenkhkare. The name Smenkhkare as shown on the ring bezels found by Petrie belonged to someone living in the city, **NOT** to a member of the Royal Family. (They were not found in the Palace.)

As I said at the start, this was where my interest was really aroused. I wondered why four different explorers could enter the same tomb and record the same cartouches, only to come out with such different results. I considered the argument that if the cartouches were gradually decaying then Robert Hay in 1830 probably saw more than Lepsius in 1845, some 15 years later. Then I wondered if perhaps the lighting or the techniques employed had developed over the course of that 15 years, and perhaps Lepsius was able to make a more accurate recording.

By concentrating on the first and last recordings I decided my research would not require the findings of the French explorers. I started with Robert Hay.

Robert Hay's work is preserved in the British Library, so armed with my Reader's Ticket I set about finding it. Robert Hay recorded his work meticulously. His drawings are as clear today as they were in 1830, and I had no problems in understanding the work he had recorded. The cartouches on the North wall of the tomb of Meryre II were still in good condition, apart from the Son of Re name of our Pharaoh and the name of his wife. When Davies published his work in 1907, the cartouches to the left of the Aten had disappeared as well as the ones we are discussing which were carved on the right. (8)

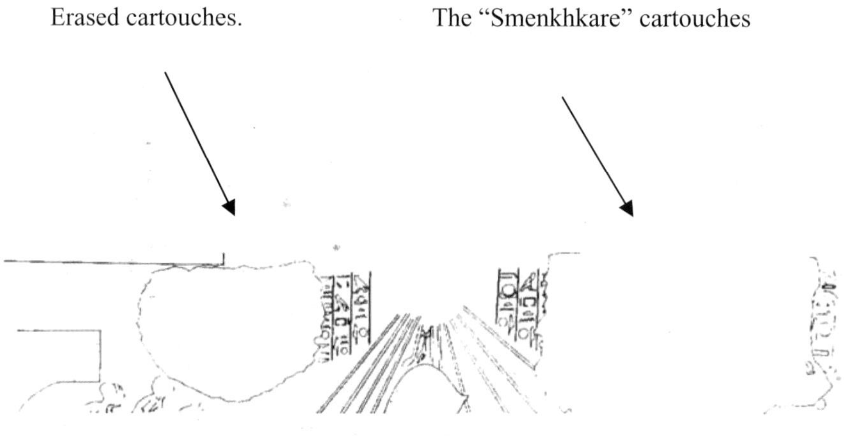

Amarna --- the missing evidence

Erased cartouches.   The "Smenkhkare" cartouches

Fig 7.5. The erased cartouches

The later names of the Aten are recorded in the first two cartouches, as is the "Lord of the two lands"  name **Ankhkheperure**. The names of the Aten would have been carved for Akhenaten, and as we have discussed, the alteration required of cartouche 3 would have been minimal. The original content of cartouches 3 and 4 would have been Akhenaten and his wife – her name being written as Neferneferuaten, and these would have required a lot of work to alter them. The cartouches are all carved with the hieroglyphs being chiselled into the rock. To overwrite them, the rock had to be flattened to make it level, and this poor quality limestone would have caused many problems. With poor lighting in the tombs and such poor quality material, it would have been stretching the limits of skilled, modern day Egyptologists to be able to say with certainty exactly what had been written. Such is the desire to "fill gaps" that over the years a Pharaoh has been created from next to nothing

Chapter 7

This is what Robert Hay actually saw. (**9**)

Fig 7.6 . Robert Hay's original work.

So, for the first time we can now see what Robert Hay saw. Pharaoh was not Smenkhkare Djeser kheper u re. There is no Djeser no plural of Kheper no men and a doubtful Khka

Pharaoh's ***nomen*** has clearly been overwritten and any reading must be considered as "best guess" here. Some of the "symbols" could easily be a piece of rough limestone.

Amarna --- the missing evidence

The cartouches can be seen more clearly by reversing the colouring:

Fig 7.7. A clearer view of Robert Hay's work.

The work of Karl Lepsius is preserved in Berlin. Scans of his work were emailed to me very promptly. (10)

Chapter 7

Lepsius did not draw his findings. He made a paper squeeze. Paper squeezes are made by first cleaning the cartouches with water. A sheet of paper is the laid over the lettering and it is beaten with a brush to ensure that the fibres of the paper fill every part of the carvings. The paper is then left to dry and peeled off, giving a mirror image of the original carving. The images below showing Lepsius' paper squeeze.

Fig 7.8 Original squeeze of Lepsius.

The paper squeeze thus show the mirror image: To make it easier to compare with the work of Robert Hay I have flipped the image horizontally.

Amarna --- the missing evidence

Fig 7.9 The cartouches in the correct order.

Lepsius does not show the s ⎯⎯ or the djeser ⌒ The Kheper is not plural | | |

This squeeze is similar to the recording of Robert Hay. The original Aten of Akhenaten 𓇋𓈖𓈗 is easy to make out, and the outline of the Ibis can be seen.

The lines of the 𓊃 s can be seen on the cartouche of the Great Royal Wife.

So where did **S men khk a re** come from? It is difficult for the modern researcher to be objective as we are presented with a wealth of information in

Chapter 7

one go. The early explorers did not have that distraction. Robert Hay was the first person to record the name of a possible successor to Akhenaten. He recorded his findings and Percy Newberry copied incorrectly.

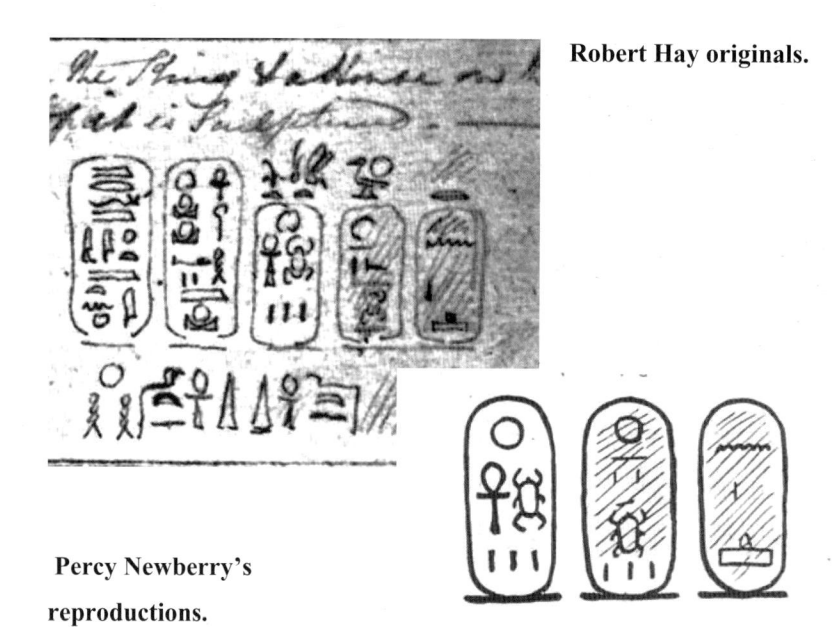

Robert Hay originals.

Percy Newberry's reproductions.

In Robert Hay;s originals it is hard to make out any symbol with certainty other than perhaps the Re at the top. Clearly the last two cartouches are badly damaged. Remember, when Newberry reproduces Hay's cartouches, he had seen the results of all four explorers and Petrie's ring bezels. Whilst the lower hieroglyph looks a bit like a kheper, I am reminded of Petrie's famous quotation:

It must be due to injury that the pile on the altar here resembles a cow !

Nine years pass before Nestor L'Hote enters the tomb. In those nine years the cartouche makes a miraculous recovery and is no longer

Amarna --- the missing evidence

damaged. The hieroglyphs are suddenly clearly visible and we have some very distinct shapes. Nestor L'Hote was an artist – a painter. His work is incredibly similar to that of Prisse D'Avennes.

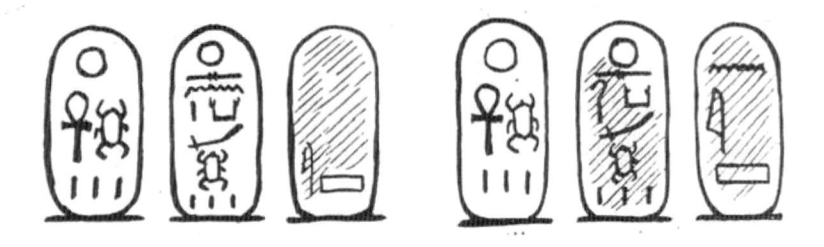

Nestor L'Hote   Prisse D'Avennes

How does this happen? In 1839 and 1843 the critical cartouche suddenly becomes clear and easy to read. This took some working out, but Norman de Garis Davies does tell us in his "Rock Tombs of Tel Amarna". (11)

I wish to modify my description of Prisse's drawings at El Amarna as reproductions of the plates of Lepsius (I., p. 4). They seem to have been originally independent drawings, often superior to Weidenbach's in detail, but Prisse, or his editor, has added to the plates every additional feature found in the Denkmuler (12) *and so has re-produced every inaccuracy of that edition.*

Newberry missed this. Remember our dates. Nestor L'Hote and Prisse D'Avennes published their work after Lepsius had published his. Lepsius in 1845,and the two French explorers in 1847. We know that Lepsius enhanced his work for publication, because we can now see the originals, and

Chapter 7

Davies admitted this when presenting the images in the Rock Tombs of Tel El Amarna.

Nestor L'Hote's work was published after his death and Prisse D'Avennes closely reproduced what Lepsius said he saw. As Nestor was not there to defend his work, it is not unlikely that his publisher sought verification in the same way.

Neither realised that Lepsius' published cartouche were not accurate and had been enhanced for publication themselves.

To summarise:

Robert Hay saw the cartouches on the North Wall of the Tomb of Meryre II before anyone else. He reported the damage to the cartouche bearing the king's nomen and to that of his wife.

Karl Lepsius visited about 15 years later, but enhanced his work for publication. Nestor L'Hote and Prisse D'Avennes altered their findings to fit Lepsius' enhanced findings. Davies followed Petrie, although Petrie's rings are not related to the tomb inscriptions.

Result: Smenkhkare

Let's take a look at our two known originals side by side.

Robert Hay   **Lepsius**

Amarna --- the missing evidence

These are not vastly different, and definitely do not read **Smenkhkare.**

If we take a look at the moment at Robert Hay's work. In the cartouche on the left, he shows Akhenaten's cartouche from another wall in Meryre II's tomb. It is quite likely that the same craftsman worked on both walls. The cartouche to the right shows the one that has been altered, which should provide Ankhkheperure's nomen.

The n at the bottom can still be seen. The curve of the t of Aten is visible, and the n from Aten, immediately below. The reed or i (pronounced a) from Aten has been erased. The Ibis now takes shape as well.

So what do we make of all this? Below the cartouches, Davies records a sketch of Pharaoh and his wife. (12) So often we are told that this must be Smenkhkare and Merytaten, but as the cartouches were unfinished,

Chapter 7

there is no reason to suppose that this is anything less than the existing drawing of Akhenaten and Nefertiti. Why look for a more complicated explanation? One thing is certain. No-one else will ever read these cartouches. This is the North Wall today.

So, what was in the centre cartouche? Did it carry the new Pharaoh's nomen? In a romantic novel there would be an answer, but unfortunately there is not one here. The work on the North Wall was rough and hurried – and probably unfinished. The **prenomen** has been altered, and sections of the name of the Royal Wife, but these were the easy bits.

Fig 7.10 The scene from the North Wall of the tomb of Meryre II

Amarna --- the missing evidence

The name "Akhenaten" has been erased after a fashion, but because of the quality of the rock and the great changes required, it is impossible to say if anything was ever carved here. The object of this chapter has been to show that this cartouche did not say "Smenkhkare". In this chapter I have shown that a Pharaoh by the name **Smenkhkare** did not exist as part of the 18th Dynasty. There is evidence to show another Pharaoh ruling alongside Akhenaten, though; a Pharaoh with the prenomen **Ankheperure** as seen in Meryre II 's tomb.

In the next chapter you will find out who that Pharaoh was.

Fig 7.11. The North wall of the Tomb of Meryre II today.

Chapter 7

Notes.

1. 1. Petrie, W M F 1896 A *History of Egypt – Part Two.* London: Methuen & Co

2. The nomen is introduced by the epithet [hieroglyph] "*son of Re*". The name in the cartouche was, as a rule, the king's name of birth. The prenomen is the name that follows the title [hieroglyph] "*King of Upper- and Lower-Egypt*".

3. Petrie, W M F., 1894 . *Tell El Amarna..* London: Methuen & Co

4. Petrie, W M F., 1894 . *Tell El Amarna..* London: Methuen & Co

5. Petrie, W M F 1896 A *History of Egypt – Part Two.* London: Methuen & Co

6. Petrie, W M F., 1894 . *Tell El Amarna..* London: Methuen & Co

7. Newberry P E,. 1928 Akhenaten's Eldest Son-in-Law, Ankhkhneprure, *Journal of Egyptian Archaeology*, 14

8. de Garis Davies, N., (1903-1908). *The Rock Tombs of El Amarna.* London: Egypt Exploration Society

9. Courtesy British Library

10. Courtesy Berlin-Brandenburgian Academy of the Sciences.

11. de Garis Davies, N., (1903-1908). *The Rock Tombs of El Amarna.* London: Egypt Exploration Society

Amarna --- the missing evidence

To conclude

Version 1 (the Established version)

Pharaoh Smenkhkare succeeded Akhenaten on the throne of Egypt.

Smenkhkare was identified by four explorers who visited the tomb of Meryre II in the 1800s and by two rings found by Petrie.

Smenkhkare is mention on several monuments, inscriptions and paintings.

Version 2 (My version)

A Pharaoh by the name Smenkhkare did not exist (Smenkhkare is a prenomen, not a nomen)

Smenkhkare was mistakenly identified by the incorrect reproduction of the four explorers to visit Meryre II 's tomb. We now have the original, reliable work.

Petrie's rings bearing the name Smenkhkare (written in two different forms) were found in the town area of Amarna.

Many more rings bearing the name Ankhkeperure were found in the palace area.

The name Smenkhkare appears on no inscription anywhere in Egypt.

You decide

Chapter 7

Challenge the Reader!   What name is/was in this cartouche?

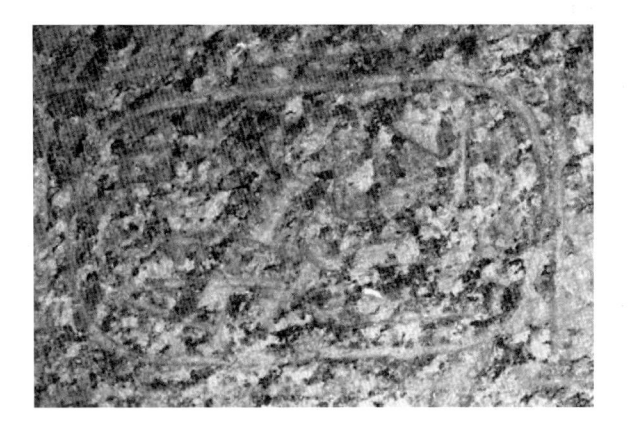

To register your solution please visit www.suemoseley.com

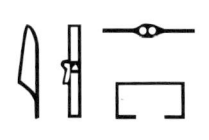

Chapter 8

Nefertiti

"The world cares very little about what a man or woman knows; it is what a man or woman is able to do that counts." --- **Booker T Washington.**

Who was Nefertiti? This has seemed to be a real problem amongst Egyptologists, and a great many opinions have been voiced. Was she a relative of Akhenaten? She never claims to be a "King's Royal Daughter". Was she the Royal Heiress? Again, she never claims to be that. There were no royal scarabs issued to proclaim the union with Akhenaten. She seems to have appeared from nowhere. It is an interesting question.

But in fact, we are clearly *told* who she was. In one of the Amarna letters, EA 28, addressed to Akhenaten, from Tushratta of Mitanni.

*To Napkhuria (**Akhenaten**), king of Egypt, my brother, my son-in-law, who loves me and whom I love, thus speaks Tushratta, king of Mitanni, **your father-in-law** who loves you, your brother. I am well. May you be well too. Your houses, Tiy your mother, Lady of Egypt, **Tadu-Heba, my daughter, your wife**, your other wives, your sons, your noblemen, your chariots, your horses, your soldiers, your country and everything belonging to you, may they all enjoy excellent health.*

Tushratta was king of the Mitanni throughout the last 12 years of the reign of Amenhotep III, and thus throughout the co-regency with Akhenaten. When Amenhotep III died, a few letters were addressed to Akhenaten, although it was clear that he still considered Queen Tiy to be in charge of her

Amarna --- the missing evidence

son. Even in the letter quoted above addressed to Akhenaten, the "Lady of Egypt" is still Queen Tiy. Tushratta was especially generous with gifts to his "brother", the Pharaoh. Once he sent a slave boy and girl along with treasures he had captured from the Hittites, and another time he sent thirty women skilled in music, needlework, and other Asiatic arts. He knew the Egyptian royal family well, and his sister was one of Amenhotep III's other wives.

Akhenaten refers to Nefertiti:
"And the Heiress, Great in the Palace, Fair of Face, Adorned with the Double Plumes, Mistress of Happiness, Endowed with Favours, at hearing whose voice the King rejoices, the Chief Wife of the King, his beloved, the Lady of the Two Lands, Neferneferuaten-Nefertiti, May she live for Ever and Always"
(From an inscription at Karnak)

Nefertiti was given the new name of Neferneferuaten by her husband, an unusual move and one that shows just how much he adored his wife. Throughout Egypt and the surrounding nations there could have been no doubt that Nefertiti was Akhenaten's true love and "Great Royal Wife." For Tushratta to say *"my daughter, your wife, **your other wives**"* can only mean that his daughter was Nefertiti.

Nefertiti's titles included:
Hereditary Princess
Great of Praises
Lady of Grace
Sweet of Love
Lady of The Two Lands
King's main wife
King's main wife, his beloved
King's great wife

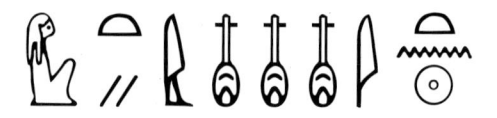

Chapter 8

King's great wife, his beloved

Lady of all Women

Mistress of Upper and Lower Egypt

This is a pretty impressive list!

Tushratta's daughter, Tadu-Heba, was sent as a young girl to join Amenhotep IIIs harem, but was clearly soon chosen by Amenhotep IV to be his wife. She probably came to Egypt around Year 26 of Amenhotep III, and was probably placed with the trusted official Aye and his wife Tiy. A year later she was chosen by Amenhotep IV to be his wife. As she was married to Akhenaten in his year 1, she was most likely to have been aged about 14 or 15 at the time.

The name Nefertiti means "The beautiful one has arrived." and was the Egyptian name given to Tada-Heba when she married Amenhotep IV. In another Amarna letter from Tushratta he mentions a second daughter Dadu-hepa – Nefertiti's sister. We meet Dadu-hepa later, and her name has become Mutnodjme which translates as "sweet mother". Mutnodjme is most frequently seen looking after her young nieces and this name would seem to have been well chosen. Mutnodjme took the role of Nurse to her young nieces.

Fig 8.1. Mutnodjme and her nieces.

Amarna --- the missing evidence

The relationships between Egypt and Mitanni had been strong for many years, and when Tushratta writes to Amenhotep III in EA 17 he greets him with:

To Nibmuaria ,(Amenhotep III) King of Egypt, my brother, say: Thus says Tushratta, King of Mitanni, your brother. It is well with me. May it be well with you; **with Kelu-Heba, my sister***, may it be well; with your household, your wives, your sons, your nobles, your warriors, your horses, your chariots, and throughout your land may it be very well.*

When I sat upon my father's throne, I was still young, and Tuhi did evil to my land, and he killed his lord. And, therefore, he did not treat me well, nor the one who was on friendly terms with me. I, however, especially because of those evils, which were perpetrated on my land, made no delay; but the murderers of Artashumara, my brother, along with all that they had, I killed.

Because you were friendly with my father, for this reason I sent and spoke to you, so that my brother might hear of this deed and rejoice. My father loved you, and you loved my father still more. And my father, because of his love, has given my sister to you. And who else stood with my father as you did? The very next year, moreover, my brother's . . . the whole land of Hatti. As the enemy came to my land, Teshub, my lord, gave him into my hand, and I destroyed him. And not one of them returned to his own land. Behold, one chariot, two horses, one male servant, one female servant, out of the booty from the land of Hatti I have sent you. And as a gift for my brother, five chariots and five teams of horses I have sent you. And as a gift for Kelu-Heba, my sister, one set of gold pins, one set of gold earrings, one gold idol, and one container of "sweet oil." I have sent her.

Behold, Keliya, my sukkal(an official) along with Tunip-ibri, I have sent. May my brother quickly dispatch them so that they may quickly bring back word so that I may hear my brother's greeting and rejoice. May my

Chapter 8

brother seek friendship with me, and may my brother send his messengers so that they may bring my brother's greeting and I may receive them.

Clearly Amenhotep III had married Tushratta's sister – Nefertiti's aunt. Although references have been found to another of Akhenaten's wives, Kiya, and some Egyptologists have argued that it is Kiya who was Tushratta's daughter this cannot be. Tushratta must have known that Nefertiti was Akhenaten's "Great Royal Wife" and adored by her husband. He would not have addressed her as among "**your other wives**". (see EA28 above)

Nefertiti married Akhenaten right at the start of his reign, and the first of six daughters soon followed. There are no images of Akhenaten anywhere that show the Pharaoh alone – his wife is always at his side. She is usually just behind her husband although often shown as a little smaller than him to start with, and from day one at Akhetaten, she is always there It is unusual to see Pharaoh's wife the same size as Pharaoh himself. The fact that Nefertiti is shown to be of equal height (proportionately) as her husband must be intentional, and must either show Nefertiti of equal importance as Akhenaten both in terms of power and religion. Nefertiti is never shown knee high as other Great Royal Wives had been depicted.

Scenes on the tomb walls show the Royal family enjoying each others company, and Akhenaten is always shown as devoted to his wife and daughters. There can be no doubt that the images found at Akhetaten are genuine reflections of life at the time. Akhenaten's art is so unusual that it has to be genuine. Akhenaten himself gave the orders to his artists. He could have ordered traditional images of Pharaohs but he chose a completely new style. It is almost as if he wanted somewhere to live where he could show the world (or at least the people of Akhetaten) just how much he adored his wife and his family. Nefertiti was the love of his life. Nothing has ever been uncovered to suggest that this devotion was not reciprocated.

Amarna --- the missing evidence

Fig. 8.2 Ramases The Great with his Great Royal Wife Nefertari standing by his right knee. Abu Simbul. Note the size of Nefertari.

Fig 8.3 Akhenaten kissing one of his daughters.

Chapter 8

A note about this little statue. (fig 8.3) It clearly shows how fond Akhenaten is of his children, yet it has been suggested that the figure seated on Akhenaten's lap is the male, Smenkhkare! If you look carefully you can still see part of the side-lock of youth which was used by the Ancient Egyptians to show that the figure was a child. This same side-lock can be seen on Akhenaten and Nefertiti's daughters throughout the tombs of the nobles at Akhetaten. This is clearly a child holding onto her father and enjoying the warmth of the hug.

Nefertiti was obviously devoted to her daughters, in particular her first born, Merytaten. Nefertiti's life could not have been easy – constantly supporting her husband and raising six daughters must have taken a great deal of time and organisation, especially in the harsh conditions of Akhetaten, yet Merytaten always appears at her side in a gesture of support.

We know very little of life at Akhetaten apart from what is shown on the walls of the tombs of the nobles. Daily rituals seemed to consist of visits to the temples and offering to the god, Aten. This monotony was occasionally broken by a special ceremony held to reward a particular noble.

The representations of Nefertiti in these daily scenes arouses a lot of interest, though. Although known throughout as "wife" which we equate to "queen", Nefertiti is quite clearly taking on the role of "king" beside her husband.

In the tomb of Aye, Nefertiti and Akhenaten are shown under the rays of the Aten beside an altar laden with offerings, and they are lifting cartouches of the Aten and statues of themselves as the twin gods Shu and Tefnut. They appear to be depicting themselves as the twin gods. Was this an attempt to elevate their status to that of being a **living** god and goddess, the son and daughter of the creator, on earth?

Amarna --- the missing evidence

Fig 8.4 Ring showing Akhenaten and Nefertiti as Shu and Tefnut. Amarna.

Fig.8.5 Akhenaten and Nefertiti as Shu and Tefnut.

Chapter 8

It is worth pausing for a moment to comment on the many scenes of apparent nudity at Akhetaten. Whilst it was not unusual for children to be shown naked, and a King is usually shown with a bare chest, it has been the cause of many comments to see Nefertiti with so few clothes on.

There are many occasions in which Nefertiti appears nude to the waist – in the royal-male manner, as Hatshepsut some years before. Sometimes it is clear that the outline of a dress, a neckline or a sleeve was intended, but there are many cases when no clothing at all is visible. This must have been intentional. Whilst we might find the Art at Akhetaten difficult to understand, there is no doubt that it was well planned. Nefertiti is shown naked to the waist **as a Pharaoh**.

There are also images of Nefertiti wearing the khat head-dress of male kings. She is shown wearing the atef crown and the khepresh crown. So, we have no records of much happening at Akhetaten, but whatever the king does, his wife can also be seen doing. In most of the "reward" scenes shown in the tombs of the nobles, the lucky men receive their gold collars from the King. In some scenes, Nefertiti is shown giving out these collars.

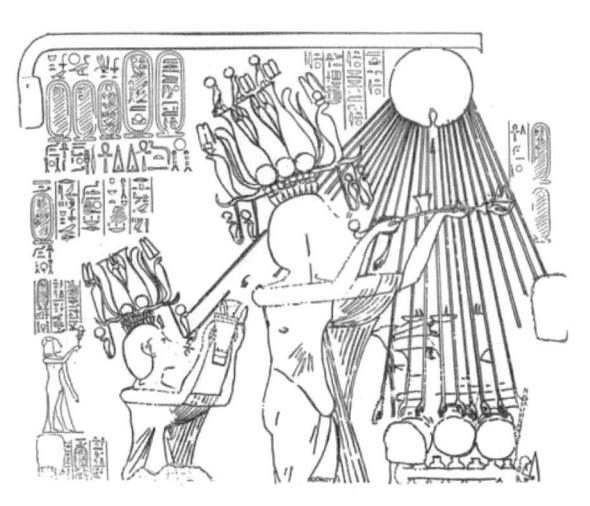

Fig. 8.6 Nefertiti wearing the Atef crown.

Amarna --- the missing evidence

There is no evidence of Akhenaten or his family leaving the city of Akhenaten, until Akhenaten visits Thebes in year 11/12, probably for his father's funeral. Life must have been pleasant, despite the hardships, as everyone appears happy in the images that remain in this fairyland city.

One of the last records of Nefertiti is an image on the wall of the tombs of Huya and Meryre II where she is seen with her husband and daughters receiving tributes from foreigners at the celebration of her husband's sole rule, or possibly in the Royal Tomb in the scenes of grief over the death of Meketaten.

Much has been made of her disappearance after year 12. We have been told that she died, or that she fell from grace to be replaced by the mysterious Kiya. There are no images of Nefertiti at Akhetaten after years 12.

There are no images of Akhenaten at Akhetaten after year 12 either!

So what happened? There is very little evidence, but it is possible to show that Nefertiti lived on as Pharaoh, having been co-regent with her husband throughout his "reign".
Remember the only visible cartouche on the North Wall of Meryre IIs tomb?

Ankh-kheper-u-re.

Bear in mind that Meryre II's tomb is the only tomb to show these cartouches, and he was **Nefertiti's steward.**

This prenomen, or throne name is often written with a feminine ending, or a letter "t" added to create a female name. **Ankh-t-kheper-u-re.** Consider too that there is no mention anywhere of a Pharaoh with the nomen Smenkhkare. The nomen associated with Ankh-kheper-u-re is **Neferneferuaten,** which had been Nefertiti's name for years.

Chapter 8

No male Pharaoh of Egypt has ever had his name spelt as a feminine name, but let's look back at one very well known female Pharaoh, Hatshepsut.

Hatshepsut's name was written in the masculine and feminine, depending on who was writing it down. Those in the know used the feminine determinative whilst others presumed that Pharaoh was a man. There is no evidence anywhere of a ***male*** Pharaoh having his name written in the feminine.

Many Egyptologists have argued that there were **two** co-regents with Akhenaten – one was Smenkhkare, using the names Ankheperure and Neferneferuaten, and the other was Nefertiti using the names Ankheperure and Neferneferuaten – but this makes no sense. As we have seen there was no Pharaoh Smenkhkare. Petrie found two rings which he registered as belonging to Smenkhkare, but as we have seen there were only two rings, each different, and found in the town areas, not the palace. These rings are lost and not available for closer inspection today.

Petrie found several unidentified rings in the town area – were their owners all Pharaohs as well?

Fig: 8.7 Some more of Petrie's rings.

So we are left with the suggestion that there were two Pharaohs with the same names. What man, about to become Pharaoh, chooses to use the names of his co-regent's wife?

Amarna --- the missing evidence

A selection of names associated with King Neferneferuaten is given below, and now show a King with a nomen and prenomen --- not two prenomens as imagined in the cartouches.

Prenomen   **Nomen**

Ankhetkheperure Mery (feminine) Waenre
                            Neferneferuaten Mery Neferkheperure- Waenre

Ankhkheperure Mery (feminine) Neferkheperure
                            Neferneferuaten the Ruler

Ankheperure Mery Neferkheperure-Waernre
                            Neferneferuaten Mery Akhenaten.

Ankheperure Mery Aten
                            Neferneferuaten Mery Waenre

Mery = beloved of

Ankh-kheper-u-re is often referred to as "beloved of Waenre" "beloved of Akhenaten" "beloved of Neferkheperure"

Of these names, clearly the first three prenomen must refer to Nefertiti – the only person ever known as "beloved of Waenre or Neferkheperure. Of the nomen, nos. 1,3 and 4 are accepted references to Nefertiti throughout the Royal Family's residence in Akhetaten. So we are left with one prenomen and one nomen to try to construct an ephemeral male Pharaoh. With no mention anywhere of a name Smenkhkare, and as Ankheperure and Neferneferuaten are established as names of Nefertiti, the case seems proven.

There is evidence that Nefertiti was Pharaoh alongside her husband throughout his reign. Only Pharaoh "smites the enemy", yet these images clearly show Nefertiti in this role. Why would these images have been painted or carved if the intention had not been to show Nefertiti as Pharaoh? No other royal wife has ever been shown performing these duties, so why should Nefertiti be shown performing them? Orders had to be given to artists to produce the images. Who gave the orders? Akhenaten? Nefertiti? Whoever gave the orders must have had a reason for giving them.

Fig. 8.8 Pharaoh Nefertiti on a royal barge "smiting the enemy"

There is a really beautiful scene showing Akhenaten with his co-regent. A relief in the Egyptian Museum, Berlin, shows two Pharaohs, both wearing the Royal Uraeus, sit sharing wine. Found at Amarna, this is clearly Akhenaten and his co-regent. There are still some who claim that the second Pharaoh is male. The intimacy of this lovely relief offers much food for thought, as if this is really a male, then everything we have seen and understood about Akhenaten must be considered as a complete sham.

The family man, devoted to his wife and children; the man who

Amarna --- the missing evidence

never leaves his wife's side; the man whose role as a father is of paramount importance; suddenly, in Year 12, becomes a homosexual. Whilst some ideas are credible, this one most certainly is not. The second Pharaoh is Nefertiti.

Fig 8.9 . The two Amarna Pharaohs.

Another image on a stelae shows our two Pharaohs in an even more intimate pose! One turns to the other with a fond "chuck" under the chin. They sit side by side under the rays of the Aten, clearly devoted to each other. So, Nefertiti ruled alongside Akhenaten, at Akhetaten. As we have seen, Life is good. Amenhotep III rules on at Thebes, the country is happy and undisturbed. It is time to step back from this blissful scene and consider what

Chapter 8

happens next. Amenhotep III eventually dies.

Images of Amenhotep III show him tired and ageing for a few years before his death, and it must have become clear to him and to Tiy that Akhenaten would not be able to rule alone, as he and had no intention of leaving Akhetaten

Fig 8.10   Pharaohs in love.

He said so on the boundary stelae back in year 5. As his mother, Tiy must have been concerned about the future.

Think for a moment how the country would react on the death of Amenhotep III. Most people had probably never even heard of Akhenaten until then, although there would be some at Thebes who remembered his early days there. What would their reaction be?

Amarna --- the missing evidence

As in any similar situation, others would be considering the problems and working on solutions. There were a number of things to consider:

1. If Akhenaten was allowed to rule alone, would he "behave" in public as a noble king of Egypt?
2. If Akhenaten was allowed to rule alone would he try to change the country's religion?
3. If Akhenaten was allowed to rule alone would he leave his playground in the desert and settle down to the more serious aspects of life as king?

The answers to all three questions were obviously "no", yet he probably had to be given a chance. Akhenaten returned to Thebes for his father's funeral, then it was back to Akhetaten to entertain the foreign guests. Nothing was changing. Something had to be done.

Akhenaten's mother, Queen Tiy, had been a frequent visitor to Akhetaten, and after her husband's death she appears to have moved there permanently. As will be seen later, there is evidence of her burial in the Royal Tomb at Akhetaten. This would have left Nefertiti free to try to hold things together elsewhere, and from the Amarna letters it would seem as if Nefertiti has let Amarna – at least for some of the time – and Merytaten takes her place beside Akhenaten. One of the last acts of Nefertiti's loyal steward, Meryre II, was to add her cartouches to a wall in his tomb. Nefertiti had finally become Pharaoh.

This all sounds very romantic, but others would have agreed that her decision to rule alone was probably not considered the best thing for Egypt. Hatshepsut's position was different. She had been queen in the same way as Nefertiti, alongside a weak Pharaoh, but she had been known to her people throughout and she was a full blooded Egyptian Royal Heiress. Hatshepsut's decision to take charge whilst Tuthmoses III was a child was considered to be a good move. Nefertiti was not known to the people of Egypt, she was of

Chapter 8

foreign birth and had spent years away from the main court, worshipping a different god.

We cannot easily construct what followed, but some theories are surely more sensible than others. Nefertiti was emulating Hatshepsut, and it seems most likely that she decided to do as Hatshepsut did. Take charge whilst the next Pharaoh was a child – in this case, Tutankhamen.

Nefertiti's highest regnal year is Year 3.

In the tomb of Pawah in Thebes the following inscription was found:

Regnal year 3, third month of Inundation, day 10. The King of Upper and Lower Egypt, Lord of the Two Lands **Ankhkheperure** *Beloved of Aten, the Son of Re* **Neferneferuaten Beloved of Waenre.** *Giving worship to Amun, kissing the ground to Wenennefer by the lay priest, scribe of the divine offerings of Amun in the Mansion of Ankhkheperure in Thebes, Pawah, born to Yotefseneb. He says:*

"My wish is to see you, O lord of persea trees! May your throat take the north wind, that you may give satiety without eating and drunkenness without drinking. My wish is to look at you, that my heart might rejoice, O Amun, protector of the poor man: you are the father of the one who has no mother and the husband of the widow. Pleasant is the utterance of your name: it is like the taste of life.

"Come back to us, O lord of continuity. You were here before anything had come into being, and you will be here when they are gone. As you caused me to see the darkness that is yours to give, make light for me so that I can see you . . .

"O Amun, O great lord who can be found by seeking him, may you drive off fear! Set rejoicing in people's hearts). Joyful is the one who sees you, O Amun: he is in festival every day!"

For the Ka of the lay priest and scribe of the temple of Amun in the Mansion of Ankhkheperure, Pawah, born to Yotefseneb: "For your Ka!

Amarna --- the missing evidence

Spend a nice day amongst your townsmen." His brother, the outline draftsman Batchay of the Mansion of Ankhkheperure.

Only one person was ever known as ***Neferneferuaten Beloved of Waenre.*** That was Nefertiti.

No mention of Smenkhkare. Pharaoh is Ankhkheperure Neferneferuaten.

Tutankhamen began his reign in Memphis, under his birth name of Tutankhaten, before moving to Thebes in year 3.

The inscription in the tomb of Pawah is the only surviving inscription outside of Akhetaten to mention Nefertiti's name in her role as King Neferneferuaten – except in Tutankhamen's tomb - and shows a reign of 3 years. Nothing more is heard of her. Nothing much is known of Tutankhamen during his 3 years in Memphis.

The Pharaoh Aye who took the throne after the death of Tutankhamen, also ruled for 3 years and lived in Thebes. Whilst there are statues and images surviving that show Aye as Pharaoh, there are no such memories of Nefertiti. This would suggest that she did not spend long in Thebes, and she probably moved there after the death of Akhenaten.

The house of **Ranofer**, the Chief Charioteer and the High Priest of Re, was built **during Nefertiti's reign,** and her cartouches were engraved over the door frame. So clearly her reign began at Akhetaten.

Plague was rife, and we have seen that plague probably kept Amenhotep III away from Thebes, so it is possible that Nefertiti died soon after moving there in her second or third year.

Akhenaten dies soon after the celebrations of year 12. He had not been visited by outsiders for 6 years and there is no doubt that plague arrived with those foreigners. No mention is made of Akhenaten or Tiy after year 12.

The only piece of evidence to set against the multitude of facts in

Chapter 8

favour of King Nefertiti is a partial shawabti of Queen Nefertiti, supposedly found at Amarna. Now at the Louvre, it has no true provenance, but is thought to have been discovered in the 1920s. It clearly gives Nefertiti's titles as "queen" which many say means that she died as a queen, not as a king. It cannot be dismissed out of hand, but must be considered against the weight of evidence in favour of her being Pharaoh. Logically, it can just as easily be explained as being a votive figure donated at the time of one of the other royal burials. There is no evidence of Nefertiti being buried at Akhenaten, as we will see in the next chapter, so if this shawabti was prepared for her own burial, what was it doing there?

And finally, another vexed question. What did Nefertiti look like? Her name and beauty were made famous by the discovery of a bust now in Berlin's Egyptian Museum .The bust is one of the most copied works of ancient Egypt. It was attributed to the sculptor Thutmose and was found in his workshop at Akhetaten by the German expedition in 1912. Widely acclaimed as a work of art, its images are sold in their thousands on T shirts, necklaces or miniature sculptures.

Unfortunately there is no **name** on the bust.

The statue was one of the last sculptures to be made before the workshop was deserted – yet Nefertiti had left Akhetaten years before. It is far more likely that the bust is actually of one of her daughters who remained in Akhetaten. Much has been made of the fact that the bust is shown without its left eye. Some have said that she must be blind. There are no other images which show Nefertiti as blind! It is far more likely that the bust was either unfinished or damaged in some way. No-one will ever know, but the bust should not be considered categorically to be that of Nefertiti. We have other images known to be of Nefertiti and none show quite this level of perfect beauty. Nefertiti means "the beautiful one has arrived", yet there are very few "beautiful" images of her.

To Akhenaten, though, she was undoubtedly beautiful.

Fig 8.11 Nefertiti bust at the Berlin Museum.

Chapter 8

To conclude

Version 1 (the Established version)
Nefertiti was disgraced towards the end of Akhenaten's rule and died before him.
Akhenaten was homosexual and took a young, unknown man to be his co-regent.
Nefertiti's image was uncovered at Amarna by the German expedition in 1912.

Version 2 (My version)
Akhenaten was utterly devoted to his wife, Nefertiti, right up to the end of his life.
Akhenaten rewarded Nefertiti with a new name, Neferneferuaten elevated her to Great Royal Wife and finally made her his co-regent.
The co-regent's name is often spelt in the feminine.
The "Bust of Nefertiti" is more likely to be the bust of one of her daughters.

You decide

Amarna --- the missing evidence

Another test:

You have been excavating at Amarna and have discovered these ring bezels in the town area.

1. Who did they belong to?
2. Are you concluding that this means they belonged to a Pharaoh?

1.   2.

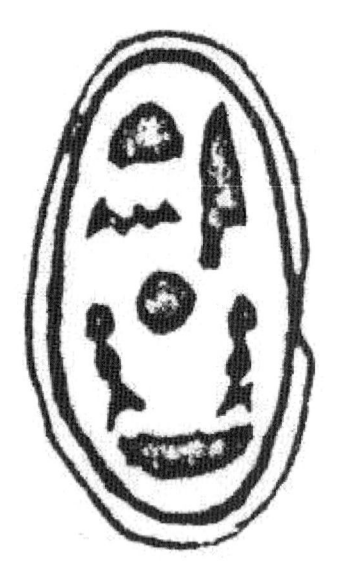

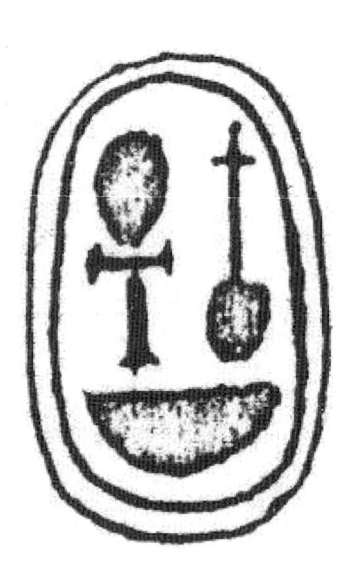

Answers please to sue@suemoseley.com

𓂉 ★ 𓅃 𓀁

Chapter 9

The Aftermath.

"In the end, we will remember not the words of our enemies, but the silence of our friends." --- **Martin Luther King.**

We are told that when Akhenaten finally died, his cartouches were erased by his successors in an effort to wipe out his memory. This was not an uncommon event. Throughout Egyptian history, Pharaohs erased the names of their predecessors and had their own names carved on top. Statues of one Pharaoh suddenly became a statue of his successor. Pharaohs often looked the same – handsome, young, strong etc. So no-one really noticed. But why did they do this?

In our modern times, if a monarch dies we simply produce new goods with the new king's name – then gradually dispose of the old. In Britain, George VI died in 1952. His initials were seen on every post-box in the country. He was succeeded by his daughter, Elizabeth II. The old boxes were not altered to show her initials. They were replaced with new ones.

So why did the Egyptian Pharaohs erase the names of their predecessors and take over their statues? It was because the Egyptians used stone. It could take years to carve a large statue and when it came to cartouches; well, wall space was limited and valuable. Pharaoh had been given a good funeral, and was well on his way to the afterlife. He had no further need for his earthly monuments. So they were re-used.

This was not some malicious act of hatred, but simply old fashioned re-cycling. In Akhenaten's case, though, his images and statues were not re-

Amarna --- the missing evidence

used. They were destroyed. This was easy to understand, though. No self respecting Pharaoh wanted to look like Akhenaten! They could not simply replace the name. New ones were called for. The same thing happened to Hatshepsut. We are told that towards the end of his reign Tuthmoses III suddenly decided he no longer liked her, and destroyed her images. Surely this was simply because he did not want his people to think he was a woman – not a vengeful act at all. It is unlikely that many Egyptians ever knew of Akhenaten. Tucked away in his city, he did not appear in public.

Fig. 9.1 George VI and Elizabeth II post boxes.

So, what became of the Amarna royal family? What became of Akhenaten, Nefertiti, Queen Tiy, the daughters? Where were they buried? Have their tombs or mummies been discovered? The answer is quite complicated as we might expect from this family!

Let's start at Akhetaten itself. One of the first decisions a new Pharaoh had to make was where he wanted to be buried. Work on the new

Chapter 9

Royal Tomb would need to be started as soon as possible as Pharaoh might die unexpectedly. Akhenaten clearly considered this delicate problem when he planned out hid new city, and the Royal Tomb was positioned in a narrow side valley, some distance from the rest of the tombs.

This Royal Tomb was discovered in the 1880s by people living in the nearby villages, and as with the Tombs of the Nobles, the rock is of very poor quality. The walls were plastered before being decorated, and as the dampness has invaded the tomb, much of the decoration has been lost. So, of the decoration, little now survives, apart from a few patches of plaster at ceiling level, with titles of the Aten, Akhenaten and Nefertiti. When the tomb was first discovered, there were scenes of women mourners from a depiction of the King's funeral. Some relics were found, the most important of these were fragments from two granite sarcophagi and their lids belonging to Akhenaten and to Meketaten. The former now stands outside the Cairo Museum.

Fragments of an alabaster canopic chest for Akhenaten was also recovered and over two hundred shawabti-figures, also belonging to Akhenaten. From this we can be fairly certain that Akhenaten was buried in the tomb when he died. Most of this burial equipment was of an entirely traditional style, including the canopic chest and shawabti-figures. These items are quite out of keeping with what we known about the worship of Aten. As Akhenaten would not have planned things this way, the decisions must have been made by those left behind. In particular, Nefertiti.

Akhenaten would have been pleased about one thing, though. From the moment he set out to plan his new city, he made it quite clear that he wanted to be buried there. The early proclamation on the Boundary stelae stated:

'Let a tomb be made for me in the eastern mountain of Akhetaten.

Amarna --- the missing evidence

Let my burial be made in it, in the millions of jubilees which the Aten, my father, has decreed for me.

So, as planned, Akhenaten was buried in his tomb, in the Eastern mountain of Akhenaten. There were early reports of the finding of human remains in the tomb, but this is impossible to verify. Where is Akhenaten's mummy? Before we consider this question, let's see what else we know about the Royal tomb. The early proclamation continues:

Let the burial of the Great King's Wife, Nefertiti, be made in it, in the millions of years which the Aten, my father, decreed for her. Let the burial of] the King's Daughter, Merytaten, be made in it, in these millions of years

His other daughters were not mentioned, simply because they had not been born, but we can assume he wanted the same end for them as well. The Royal Tomb was built with several chambers, which would suggest it was built for different family members. As no-one can know who is going to die first it would seem most likely that the chambers were built and not decorated until they were required for use.

Chamber Alpha was decorated for an un-named princess. Akhenaten and Nefertiti bend over the body of a woman, weeping and gripping each other's arms for support. Nearby a nurse stands with a baby in her arms, accompanied by a fan-bearer, which indicates the baby's royal status. The names in the scene have been lost.

Much has been written about these two chambers, and it is worth considering what the scenes tell us. Some say that the scenes in Chamber Alpha were also of Meketaten, but this seems unlikely. Each chamber was clearly carved, then left to be decorated when a member of the royal family

Chapter 9

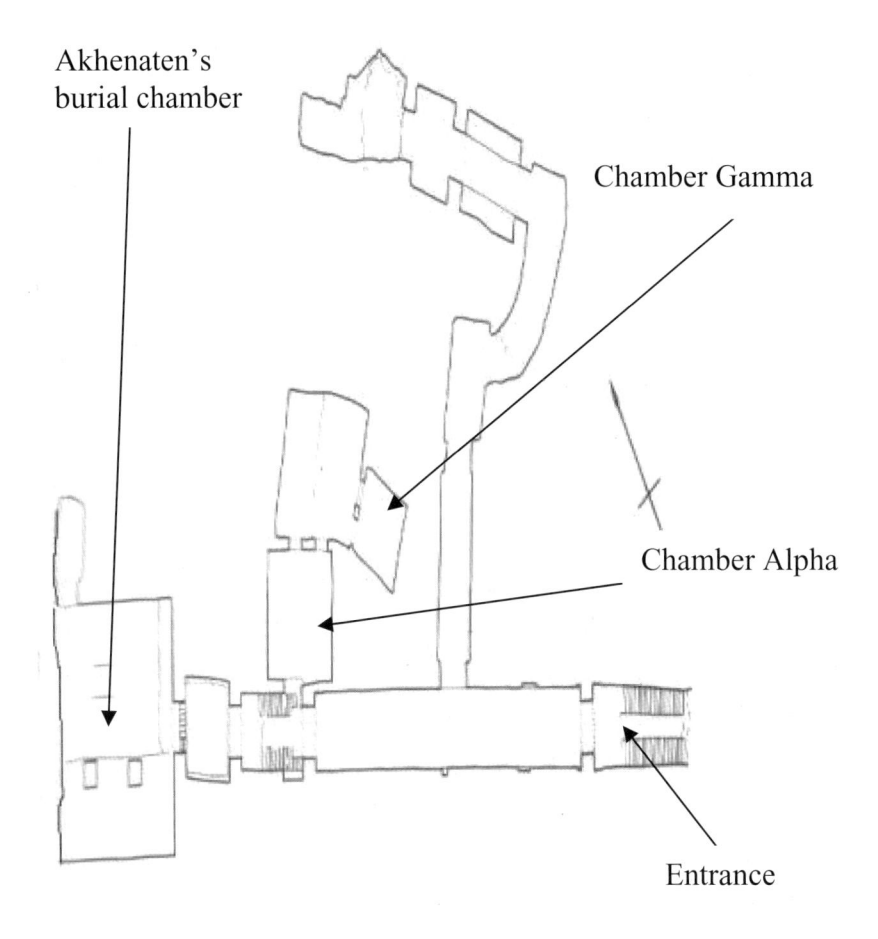

Fig. 9.2 Plan of the Royal Tomb

Chamber Gamma shows similar scenes, but in this tomb the princess is named as Meketaten the second daughter of the royal family.

Amarna --- the missing evidence

Fig. 9.3 Chamber Alpha

Fig. 9.4 Chamber Gamma

Chapter 9

This theory goes further to suggest that the baby who is being taken from the chamber by a nurse is really Tutankhamen! It makes for an interesting theory but is most unlikely.

The men who decorated the tombs at Akhetaten were either following orders or were sadly lacking in imagination as many of the scenes are used over and over again with little variation. I have used the words "mass produced" for a reason. These two scenes are so similar that they must have been used to depict the same event, albeit a different person. The scenes are of incredible grief, and in Chamber Gamma we know that grief is for Princess Meketaten. The scenes in Chamber Alpha must depict the death of another daughter. But which one?

We know that the third daughter Ankhesenpaaten outlived the entire family. She went on to marry Tutankhamen who was buried in the Valley of the Kings. So it is unlikely that she was returned to Akhetaten for burial. That leaves Merytaten, the oldest daughter, or one of the younger children, Neferneferuaten, Neferure or Setepenre. Merytaten was alive late into the reign of Akhenaten, and was possibly the one who supported Nefertiti when she became Pharaoh. When Tutankhamen's tomb was discovered, a statue of Anubis was found. This beautiful statue, and between its paws was a palette. Two inscriptions in the lower part of this palette show that it was made for Tutankhamen by the 'Princess Merytaten, daughter of the Great Royal Wife Nefertiti'.

Was Merytaten still alive when Tutankhamen's tomb was furnished? If so, then hers was not the occupant of Chamber Alpha. It would seem most likely, then, that the un-named princess was one of the younger children, born after Year 8 of Akhenaten's reign

Fig.9.5 The Anubis Statue from the Tomb of Tutankhamen.

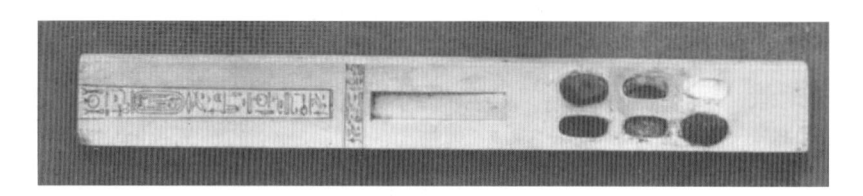

Fig. 9.6 The Palette between Anubis' paws.

As Akhenaten is clearly alive at her burial, the scene must be around Year 12, when the oldest age for the daughter could be four! By Year 12, Meketaten would have been 9. As a Teacher, I have known 11 year old girls become pregnant, but 9 year olds is a bit unlikely! The girl would have had to

Chapter 9

conceive the baby at 8 years old. We won't even entertain the idea of the 4 year old!

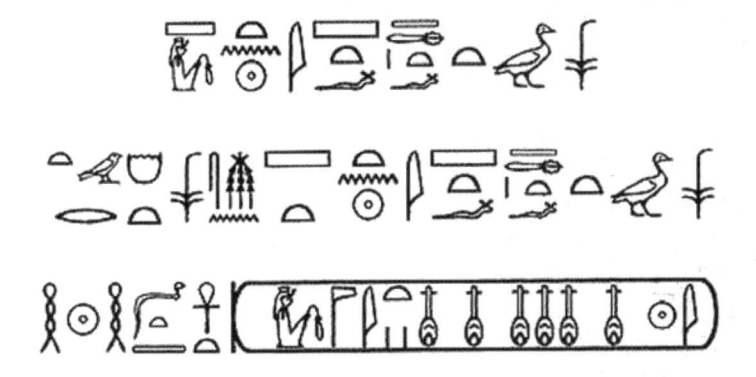

Fig. 9.7 The inscription on the Palette

So where does that leave the interpretation of the scene in chamber Alpha, showing the nurse leaving with a royal baby?

Fig. 9.8 The nurse leaving Chamber Alpha, carrying a royal baby.

Amarna --- the missing evidence

The ancient Egyptians believed that each person's "ka" came into existence at the moment of birth. It is difficult for us to understand the literal meaning of "ka" but it was an essential ingredient which differentiated a living person from a dead one. Although everyone would eventually die, the "ka" would live on to ensure eternal life.

It is just possible to make something of the cartouche in front of the nurse.

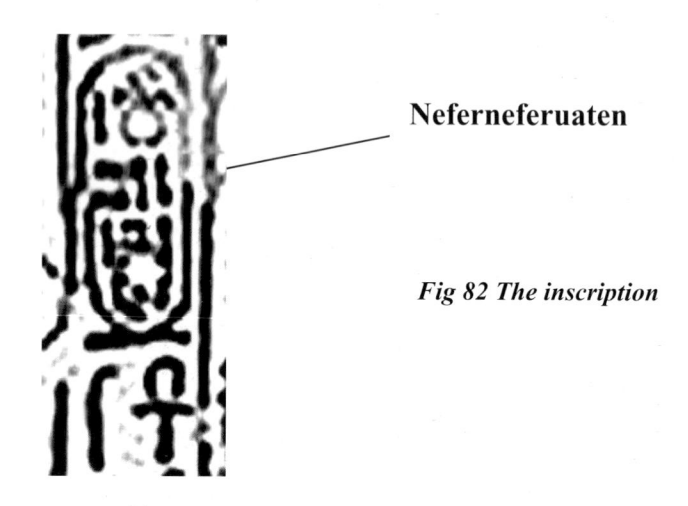

Neferneferuaten

Fig 82 The inscription

Akhenaten's religion was different to other religions, in that there were no images of religious symbols. This is surely the way the "ka" is interpreted at Akhetaten under the new religion. The inscription must read "born of the Great Royal Wife Neferneferuaten" and was simply a way of showing that the Princess would live on. Her "ka" was leaving her body.

Akhenaten is clearly the father of both princesses, as the scenes are so similar. It is unlikely that the very real and intense feelings of grief shown by Nefertiti would have been called for if the scene in Chamber Alpha was showing the death of another of her husband's wives!

So, Akhenaten and two of his daughters were buried in the Royal Tomb. One of the younger daughters married King Niqmat of Ugarti. The

Chapter 9

two youngest daughters are not shown in the scenes of grieving for Meketaten so one of these could be the bride in question.

Fig. 9.9 Fragment found at Ugarti showing the marriage of the King Niqmat to an Amarna Princess.

Which leaves three unaccounted for. More about Ankhesenpaaten in the next chapter, which leaves two. It is possible that more daughters were buried in the royal tomb, but we have no way of knowing. There are unfinished chambers in the tomb, and other tombs have been discovered at Akhetaten which were probably intended for royal burials.

So what of Queen Tiy? As traces of two sarcophagi were found in the Royal burial chamber, it is most likely that Tiy was buried there, before

Amarna --- the missing evidence

the death and burial of her son. And Nefertiti? Well, it would be wrong to look for her at Akhetaten. Nefertiti left Akhetaten to live in Thebes, so she must have been buried there. If she died of natural causes or disease, then she should be buried in the Valley of the Kings and no doubt her tomb will be discovered in the future. If she was murdered, then her final resting place may never be known. No mummies were never found in the Royal Tomb, so where did they go?

"On New Year's Day, January 1st 1907, the excavation work in the Valley of the Kings, supervised by a well-to-do American Theo M Davis, had to be delayed, the obstacle being a huge heap of rubble at the foot of the cliffs. Beyond it, scattered along the tawny hillsides, were entrances to royal tombs, gaping caves in the ground" **(1)**

Tomb KV55 had been discovered and it has caused controversy ever since. Davis was convinced that he had discovered the tomb of Queen Tiy. The passageway was blocked by the folds of a door covered in gold foil, and on the door were scenes of a queen worshipping the Aten. The team deciphered the name of Queen Tiy on the door. Her name was found on other parts of the shrine, but when Davis examined the wooden coffin, there were no names at all. The names had been erased. The coffin had actually carried the name of a King, not a Queen, and the mummy carried a gilded uraeus and gilded wooden beard. In a recess above the coffin were four alabaster canopic jars with stoppers carved as human heads. Each head had originally carried a royal uraeus which had been snapped off. Four "magic bricks" were found in the tomb, bearing the name of --- **Akhenaten.**

So who was buried in the tomb? Two doctors who happened to be in the area were asked to examine the mummy, and they declared it to be female. Davis was convinced he had found the tomb of Queen Tiy and despite the fact that Elliot Smith, Professor of Anatomy in Cairo later decided

Chapter 9

that the remains were those of a male aged 25-26, Davis went on to publish a report under the title "The Tomb of Queen Tiyi"

What else can the coffin tell us? In 1957, Sir Alan Gardiner, the leading authority on Egyptian antiquities, published an article in the Journal of Egyptian Archaeology entitled "The so-called coffin of Queen Tiye." In this article he pointed out that is was the custom in the 18th Dynasty to inscribe the foot end of a sarcophagus with the address by the goddess Isis to her brother/husband Osiris, the god of the dead. As Akhenaten did not recognise these gods, it was only his wife, Nefertiti, who could inscribe the foot end to Akhenaten. As the name of the woman addressing the king had been erased from the coffin in this tomb, Gardiner regarded this as evidence that the coffin belonged to Akhenaten.

In 1966 R.G.Harrison, Derby Professor of Anatomy at the University of Liverpool produced a report entitled An Anatomical Examination of the Pharaonic remains purported to be Akhenaten. Because of the age of the mummy and given the information he had at the time, he presumes the mummy to be Smenkhkare and writes:

"There is no doubt that Smenkhkare and Tutankhamen were closely related to one another, perhaps as brothers --- as will be demonstrated later, there are certain physical resemblances between them." Later in the report:

"Such a resemblance between the present remains and Tutankhamen has already been suggested on anatomical grounds by Derry, who found such a close correspondence between the measurements of the skull of the remains and the head of Tutankhamen as to proclaim that they were brothers ---" **(2)**

The mummy found in KV55 and Tutankhamen ***were*** brothers, as you can see in chapter 10. It was not the mummy of Smenkhkare though! The mummy was that of Akhenaten. The actual cartouches on the coffin had been erased, but the length of the cartouche gives a clue as to whose name was originally inscribed. It was a long cartouche which bore his name.

Amarna --- the missing evidence

Peperpelkin, who wrote a detailed description of the Golden Coffin concludes his work by saying:
"there is not a shadow of doubt that the burial was Pharaonic. The coffin was meant to represent a swaddled mummy of the dead king, since his forehead was adorned with a uraeus, and the long narrow beard of Egyptian male deities was attached to his chin. --- The didactic name of the sun, inscribed on the axis of the neck of the uraeus, together with the coffin inscriptions, make it certain that the coffin dates back to the Amarna Period." **(1)**

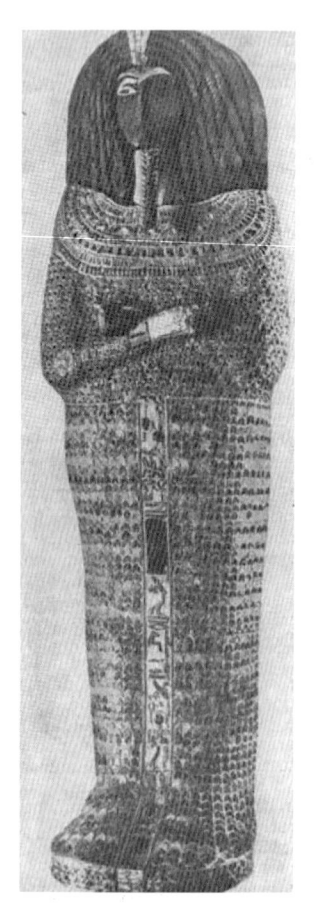

Fig 9.10 The Golden Coffin from KV55

Chapter 9

Fig. 9.11 One of the canopic jars found in tomb KV55

Arthur Weigall, who was Inspector General of the Antiquities of Upper Egypt at the time of the discovery of tomb KV55 had very strong views on the identity of the mummy. In his article in the Journal of Egyptian Archaeology, he describes bands which were discovered with the mummy. These bands ran up the length of the mummy and down again to the foot; and around the width of the mummy. These appear to have been lost soon after the tomb was emptied. At the end of his article, Arthur Weigall writes:

To sum up:- the mummy lay in the coffin of Akhenaten, was enclosed in bands inscribed with Akhenaten's name, and was accompanied by the canopic jars of Akhenaten. It was a man of Akhenaten's age, the facial structure corresponds to the portraits of Akhenaten, and it has physical characteristics similar to those of Akhenaten's father and grandfather. How, then, can one possibly doubt its identity?" **(3)**

Amarna --- the missing evidence

So what of the age of the mummy? According to several examinations it was aged about 25 to 26. Elliot Smith came to this conclusion, but added "no anatomist would be justified in refusing to admit that this individual may have been several years younger or older than this estimate."

How old was Akhenaten when he died? In the biography of Bokenkhons, High Priest of Amun under Ramases II, we are told that "personages came of age at 16." So if Akhenaten's year 1 was when he was 16, and he died in year 13, he would have been 29 when he died.

The Gold Coffin may not have been made for Akhenaten, but there can be no doubt that the men who put the coffin into the tomb believed that the mummy inside was his. The problem in the past has been in the age of the mummy. If Akhenaten had ruled for 17 years he would have been at least 33 at the time of his death. Akhenaten did not rule for 17 years, though. Having decided that Akhenaten would have been too old to be the mummy in the coffin, the old question "if not him, then who?" was voiced. A dangerous question, but one that led straight away to the assumption that it must be Smenkhkare. With no evidence at all that a male by the name Smenkhkare succeeded Akhenaten, this was the only name that could be thought of – so it must be "him."

The seals on the doors of KV55 were Tutankhamen's necropolis seals. consisting of a jackal over nine bound captives. So it would seem that the gold coffin was put into the tomb during his reign. Akhetaten was still occupied, but no-one from the royal family lived there. The time had come to move Akhenaten to the Valley of the Kings. As Tutankhamen was a mere child, the decision was not his, and as he began his reign in Memphis the most likely candidate is Nefertiti. She was living in Thebes as Pharaoh in charge while Tutankhamen was so young – it seems most logical that it was she who moved her husband. She probably moved Queen Tiy as well,

Chapter 9

although it seems that at some time later she was moved again, to be re-united with her husband in his tomb.

The discovery of unnamed female mummy in the cache in the tomb of Amenhotep II has recently been identified as Queen Tiy, so it does seem as if she was moved from KV55 to join Amenhotep III in his tomb in the Western Valley.

And the burning question --- *where was Nefertiti buried?*

She was Pharaoh, living in Thebes, so she should have found a final resting place in the Valley of the Kings. With power struggles continuing throughout Egypt, it is to be hoped that she did receive a burial fit for such a lady. There are undiscovered tombs still in the Valley, so maybe one day we will know. Until then, it is left to the speculators.

Notes

1. Perepelkin, G., 1978 *The Secret of the Golden Coffin* Moscow
2. Harrison, R G.,1966 **An Anatomical Examination of the Pharaonic Remains Purported to be Akhenaten**, *Journal of Egyptian Archaeology* 52
3. Weigall, A., 1922 *Journal of Egyptian Archaeology* 8

Amarna --- the missing evidence

To conclude:

Version 1 (the Established version)

Nefertiti died before Akhenaten and was buried at Akhetaten.
Kiya, a secondary queen, also died and was buried in the royal tomb.
Nefertiti is shown weeping over her corpse.
Kiya died in childbirth, and Tutankhamen is being carried out of the tomb.
Smenkhkare was buried in tomb KV55

Version 2 (My version)

There is no evidence of the burial of Nefertiti at Akhenaten.
The scenes of grief attributed to Kiya are actually scenes of grief over one of the royal daughters.
The daughters did not die in childbirth.
Akhenaten was buried in KV55.

You decide

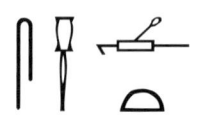

Chapter 10

Tutankhamen and Aye

"Uneasy lies the head that wears a crown." --- **William Shakespeare**

This chapter is not the story of Tutankhamen and his life. Many excellent books have already been written on this subject and I cannot hope to do justice to his biography in one chapter. My aim here is to examine just a few aspects of the story, and try to explain them using my now well established holistic approach. Given that the Pharaohs of Egypt lived unusual lives, there are still certain human aspects which have not been well explained.

Tutankhamen is probably the most famous Pharaoh of all time, thanks to Howard Carter who discovered his tomb in the Valley of the Kings in 1922. The tomb was comparatively undisturbed by robbers and has provided Egypt with some of its most famous treasures. Whilst overwhelmed by the amount and quality of the treasure, Howard Carter was disappointed in the finds. More than anything else he had hoped to find documents that would cast a new light on events in the late 18th Dynasty. But there was nothing. His life was as much a mystery after the discovery of the tomb as it was before.

"The mystery of his life still eludes us – the shadows move but the dark is never quite dispersed." Howard Carter

Even without detailed paperwork, though, one vital piece of information was uncovered. An examination of Tutankhamen's mummy gave an age at death of 18. As the highest known year of his reign was 9, it could

Amarna --- the missing evidence

be concluded that he came to the throne at the age of about 9. Another child king – a pawn in someone's power struggle maybe. Another interesting piece of information found in the tomb was that Tutankhamen started his reign as Tutankh- **aten**. A child of the Amarna age. But whose child?

The most popular theory at the moment is that he was the son of Kiya and Akhenaten. Kia was the minor wife, and this theory holds that it was Kiya's death shown in the scenes in Room Alpha in the Royal Tomb. The child being carried out was Tutankhamen. (fig. Chapter 9)

As we have seen, the cartouche in front of the baby reads Neferneferuaten not Tutankhaten, and the full inscription reads

"' [...] born of [...] Neferneferua[ten] Nefertiti, who lives now and forever more'". This is the dead daughter's Ka leaving her body.

So, if Kiya was not Tutankhamen's mother, who was? Before we consider mother, let's consider father, as that is much more straightforward.

A block which it is believed originated at Akhetaten records that Tutankhamen was the son of a King. Immediately the field narrows. The only two possible "kings" are Amenhotep III and Akhenaten. Egyptian Pharaohs are notoriously bad at giving details of their sons. Daughters – yes, no problems, but sons? Very secret and private. This has often made it difficult to track a father unless the son tells us who his parents were. Well, Tutankhamen does tell us who his father was – but he is rarely believed!

In an inscription at the Temple of Sulb in Nubia, Tutankhamen does refer to Amenhotep III as his father and Tuthmoses IV as his grandfather. So why do we continue to argue in favour of Akhenaten as his father? It can only be because it makes a more romantic story, but as the father determines the sex of his child, and as Akhenaten fathered six daughters by Nefertiti, it does seem as if he had problems producing a male heir.

The argument has been put forward that as Tutankhamen would not have been able to mention Akhenaten's name in public, he chose instead to

Chapter 10

link himself to his grandfather, Amenhotep III. If Akhenaten was his father, then he would have been born in year 3 of his father's reign, while the family still lived at Thebes. There is no mention of Kiya before the move to Akhetaten, and even there her name does not appear until late in the reign.

We have compared Akhenaten to Henry VIII earlier in this book, and there is an uncanny similarity again. Henry VIII could not father healthy sons. No matter how hard he tried, and Henry VIII certainly tried with six wives, his sons either died very young or lived on as boys with poor health. His daughters were strong and healthy. It would seem that Akhenaten faced the same problems – and we can go back a generation to see its origins. Amenhotep III fathered strong, healthy daughters, but his two boys (three if we count Tuthmose who died young anyway) were weak. Akhenaten clearly had "problems" and Tutankhamen is mostly shown sitting down being tended by his wife or walking with a stick. He died aged 18.

If we accept that Amenhotep III was Tutankhamen's father, then let's go back to his mother. We know that Tutankhamen lived at Akhetaten for a few years, and we know that Queen Tiy and her daughter Beketaten moved to live there – so it is quite likely that Tutankhamen moved there with her as well. Tutankhamen's parents were most likely to have been Amenhotep III (as he tells us) and his wife, Queen Tiy. The problem with this is that it is not quite such a romantic story as a secondary wife who dies in childbirth, but it is the most logical decision to make.

So, when Amenhotep III dies, and with Akhenaten trying to go it alone, the thoughts of many must have turned to the next in line to the Throne – Akhenaten's younger brother – Tutankhamen.

Referring back to chapter 9, we have established that the two were indeed brothers. Tutankhamen began his reign as a 9 year old boy. He moved initially to Memphis where he ruled under his birth name Tutankhamen, and as we have seen, he stayed in Memphis for three years. Nefertiti –

Amarna --- the missing evidence

Ankheperure Neferneferuaten – was his regent, but as she moved to Thebes, a loyal servant was sought to look after him. That man was Horemheb. He may have been chosen because of his earlier service to the Royal Family at Akhetaten – known then as Pa aten m heb, but it is hard to be sure. Whilst an excellent choice, it might have been Nefertiti's eventual downfall.

In Year 3 of Tutankhamen's reign, when he was still a boy at the age of twelve and probably under the influence of his older advisor Horemheb, the capital was moved back to Thebes. The young Pharaoh adopted the name Tutankhamen, changing it from his birth name Tutankhaten. We must remember that because of his age at the time, these decisions were made by his advisors – mostly by Horemheb. A Restoration stelae was built at Thebes, which has been the subject of much debate ever since.
The stelae was inscribed with the usual words of Pharaoh, followed by:

"Now when his majesty appeared as king, the temples of the gods and goddesses from Elephantine down to the marshes of the Delta had fallen into neglect. Their shrines had become desolate, had become mounds overgrown with weeds. Their sanctuaries were as if they had never been. Their halls were a footpath. The land was topsy-turvy and the gods turned their backs upon this land. --- His majesty made monuments for the gods by making their holy statues of genuine electrum of the best of the foreign lands He recreated their sanctuaries as monuments until the limits of eternity, exquisitely equipped with offerings for all eternity, by endowing them with divine offerings as regular daily sacrifices and endowing them with provisions on earth."

It would imply that the temples of Amun had suffered badly during the reign of Akhenaten, and that he had suppressed the ancient religions. Our evidence shows that this is simply not the case. On his own Coronation stelae, some 10 years later, Horemheb claims: ***to have renewed the god's***

Chapter 10

mansions and fashioned all their images --- Re rejoiced when he saw them – they having been found wrecked from an earlier time..

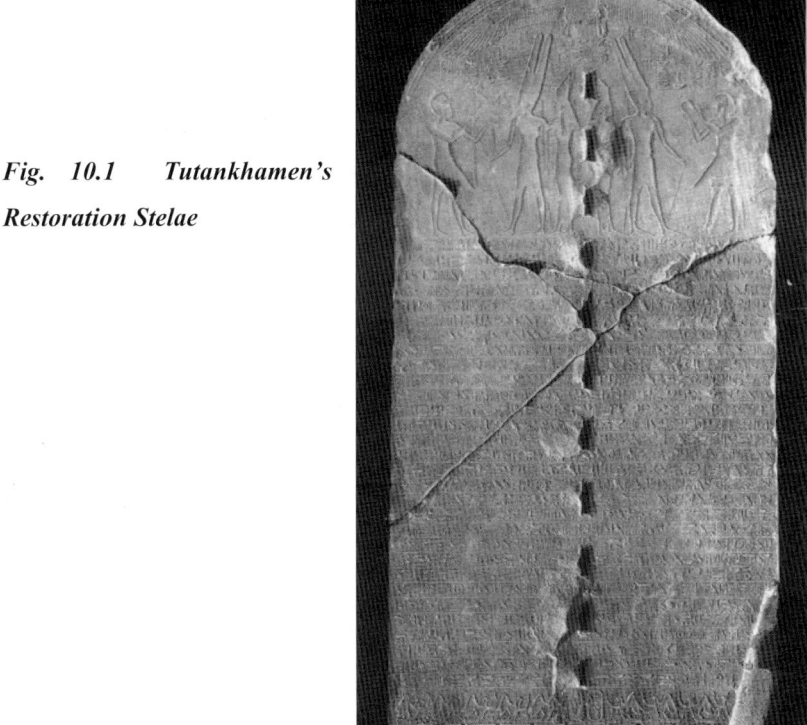

Fig. 10.1   Tutankhamen's Restoration Stelae

Were the temples *still* in need of restoration? Ten years after Tutankhamen made his declarations to put things right? If there was any damage to the temples of Amun then surely it would have been recorded somewhere? The people of Egypt would have been furious, yet no mention is ever made of such a major event? Pharaohs of the 19th Dynasty occasionally mentioned Akhenaten, although never by name. They referred to him as the

Amarna --- the missing evidence

"rebel". Nothing stronger – not the "destroyer" or "vandal." This is strange if he had really destroyed the sacred temples of Amun. So how do we explain Tutankhamen's Restoration stelae?

Tutankhamen's inscription describes their lot as one of total destruction. Unfortunately, as we all know, rulers everywhere, have been known to embellish the truth, make themselves and their actions seem more important, detract from their enemies' worth, claim the achievements of others as their own or simply copy somebody else's inscriptions. Pharaohs were no different to modern rulers in this respect. We should remember that the stelae's statements are very general and largely unsupported by independent evidence.

A king who needed the support of the priesthood might well have talked of the 'desolation of the shrines' to make his own contribution to the temples more impressive. We know that the worship of other gods went on even in Akhetaten itself. Amulets and figurines of Hathor, Isis, Bes, the *wedjat* and even inscriptions bearing the name of Amen have been found there.

Horemheb's Coronation Stelae shows that the words should not be taken too literally. Another, and possibly most interesting unanswered question about Tutankhamen's life is "How did he die?" Everyone loves a conspiracy theory, and when Tutankhamen's skull was finally x-rayed, the speculations ran rife. The x-ray showed a small piece of bone dislodged at the top of the skull, so --- was he murdered? Who killed him? Did he fall out of his chariot? There were many and varied theories about how the piece of bone was dislodged until someone suggested the obvious. As part of the mummification process different organs are removed from the body and stored in canopic jars ready for use in the afterlife. The brain was removed by hooking it out down the nose. Not very pleasant but it is unlikely that he

Chapter 10

complained. The small piece of bone in question was most likely dislodged by the hook.

So no real mystery there. Normal 18 year olds do not just die, though, unless by some fatal disease or from inherited infirmity. In Britain Henry VIII's only son Edward VI died from tuberculosis at age 15 having been a weak child. Representations of Tutankhamen do not show him to have been robust. Many show him with a walking stick, or with Ankhesenamen tenderly leaning forward towards him in an attitude more fitting of a mother than a wife. So perhaps he was suffering from a genetic disorder.

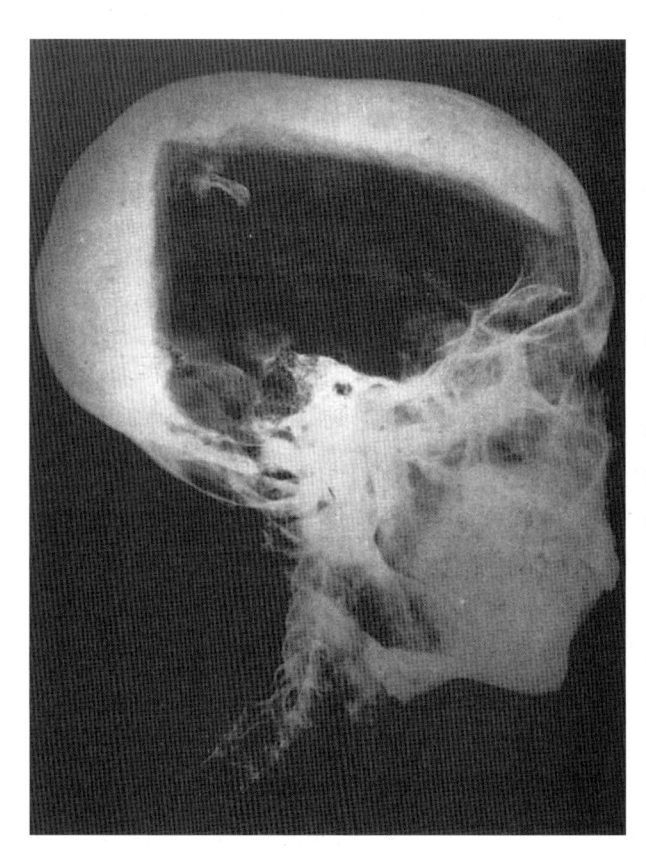

Fig.10.2 The x-ray of Tutankhamen's skull, showing the loose bone at the back.

Amarna --- the missing evidence

We know that plague and disease were widespread. Did Tutankhamen fall victim to that? With two perfectly reasonable explanations for the death of this young man, it is pure speculation to look for a more sinister reason. One day medical technology and the Egyptian Authorities might combine forces and examine Tutankhamen's mummified remains once more. Maybe then we will know.

When Tutankhamen dies, a surprise figure takes the throne. The elderly "God's Father" Aye. At the time of Tutankhamen's death, Egypt was engaged in a fairly major battle with the Hittites that ended in a defeat at Amqa not far from Kadesh. Though we do not know whether Horemheb was leading the Egyptian troops in this battle, he does not appear to have been much involved in Tutankhamen's funerary arrangements, despite his high position. This may suggest that he was out of the country at this time. If that was the case then perhaps Aye took advantage of the situation. Horemheb had been ruling the country for the past ten years and was ambitious – he would surely have taken the throne had he been around. That Aye made a quick and decisive decision can be seen on one of the walls of Tutankhamen's burial chamber. It is Aye, already Pharaoh, who performs the "opening of the mouth" ceremony. This is the only example ever found of the succeeding Pharaoh performing this ceremony.

The mummified foetuses of two mis-carried girls were found in Tutankhamen's tomb – presumably his daughters. So there was no direct heir to the throne and it is doubtful if Tutankhamen had nominated a successor – although of course he might have nominated Aye.

Aye ruled for a maximum of 3 years. In 1920 Percy Newberry claimed to have found a ring in Cairo with the cartouches of Aye and Tutankhamen's widow, Ankhesenamen side by side.

Chapter 10

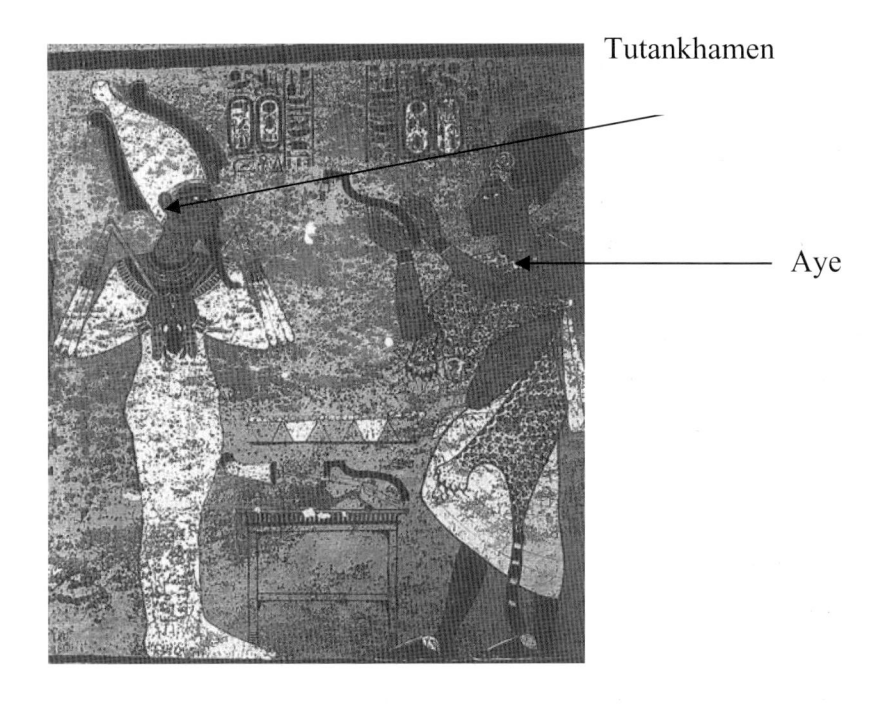

Fig 10.3. Aye performing the Opening of the mouth ceremony in the tomb of Tutankhamen.

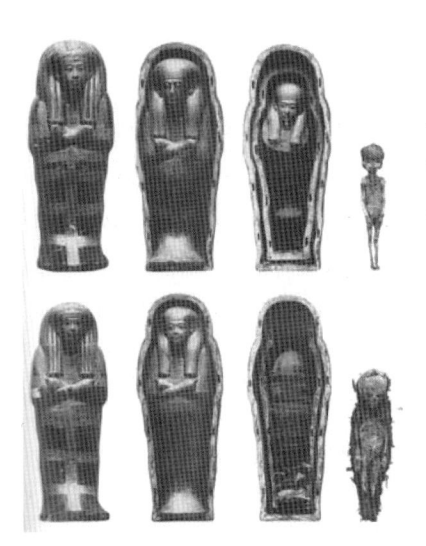

Fig.10.4 The coffins and mummified remains of Tutankhamen's two daughters.

Amarna --- the missing evidence

It was assumed that the two had married to legitimise Aye's claim to the throne. There was no provenance to the ring, though, and has since been lost; so it is difficult to treat it as a trustworthy piece of evidence. Aye does not mention Ankhesenamen as his wife in his tomb. He only mentions the wife we saw with him at Amarna. His wife Tiiy.

We do not know what happened to Ankhesenamen but there is just one last interesting piece of speculation. Suppiluliuma was the King of the Hittites around this time. (although many have tried, the uncertainty of dates makes exact matches impossible.) His son, Mursilli wrote his fathers memoirs and recorded an interesting event.

"But when the people of Egypt heard of the attack on Amka, they were afraid. And since, in addition, their lord Nibjuruiya had died, therefore the queen of Egypt, who was Dabammanzu?, sent a message to my father and wrote to him thus: "My husband died. A son I have not. But to thee, they say, the sons are many. If thou wouldst give me one son of thine, he would become my husband. Never shall I pick out a servant of mine and make him my husband! --- I am afraid."" **(2)**

Now this makes a lovely story! A young, proud queen desperate to keep her throne, seeking a husband to help her achieve this. At first, it was thought that the queen in question was Nefertiti, but the latest theories are that *Nibjuruiya* is more closely translated as Neb-kheper-u-re or Tutankhamen. His widow was Ankhesenamen.

The name *Dabammanzu* does not help a lot, but could be very loosely translated as: "queen". The test does seem to imply that a name is being given, though :

the queen of Egypt, **who was** *Dabammanzu*

Nevertheless it is an interesting story. Perhaps Egyptian history would have changed if Suppiluliuma had responded quickly --- but he didn't. Mursilli continues:

Chapter 10

"When my father heard this he called forth the Great one for council (saying) "Such a thing has never happened to me in my whole life!"" **(2)**

Suppiluliuma sent scout Hattusaziti to Egypt to see if the story was true. He did not trust Dabammanzu, and thought it might be a trap.

The next part of the story causes concern.

"But when it came Spring, Hattusaziti (came back) from Egypt and the messenger of Egypt came with him. Now since my father had, when he sent Hattusaziti to Egypt, given him orders as follows: "Maybe they have a son of their lord! Maybe they deceive me and do not want my son for the kingship!" --- therefore the queen of Egypt wrote back to my father thus: "Why didst thou say "they deceive me" in that way? Had I a son would I have written about my own and my country's shame to a foreign land? Thou didst not believe me and hast even spoken thus to me! He who was my husband has died. A son I have not! Never shall I take a servant of mine and make him my husband! I have written to no other country, only to thee have I written! They say thy sons are many; so give me one son of thine! To me he will be my husband, but in Egypt he will be king!"" **(2)**

According to Mursilli, Suppiluliuma finally agrees to send a son, who is promptly killed by the Egyptians before he gets far into the country. But the story does not really hold true. According to Egyptian custom, just 70 days are allowed between death and burial. In no more than 70 days after the death of Tutankhamen, Aye was Pharaoh. He is shown as Pharaoh on the wall of Tutankhamen's tomb. Ankhesenamen knew this, so as time was of such vital importance, why only write to one country!

Ankhesnpaaten also knew that she had only a tentative claim to the throne. She may have been the last surviving daughter of Akhenaten and with no other heirs it seems she could have made a case for the throne to go to her. She was unlikely to succeed, though, and even less likely with a Hittite husband. So why did she write to Suppiluliuma?

Amarna --- the missing evidence

Well of course we do not know that she did! Mursilli writes his father's memoirs – second hand evidence and not from personal experience. The name Dabammanzu is not Egyptian, so although the romantic story of a desperate widow makes fine reading, it must be read with a certain scepticism. Was Aye the "servant" referred to? Did Aye feel that a marriage with Ankhesenamen would make his claim to the throne stronger? If he did marry her then he kept it very quiet as there are no records of such a union.

Notes:

1. Murnane, WJ.,1995 *Texts from the Amarna Period in Egypt.* Atlanta Scholars Press
2. Guterbock, HG., 1956 The Deeds of Suppiluliuma as told by his son, Mursilli II. *Journal of Cuneiform Studies,*

Conclusion

To conclude:

Version 1 (the Established version)

Tutankhamen came to the throne after Smenkhkare.

Tutankhamen restored the temples of Amun after the destruction in Akhenaten's reign.

Tutankhamen started his reign at Akhetaten and moved to Thebes in year 3.

Tutankhamen was probably murdered.

Version 2 (My version)

Tutankhamen came to the throne after the death of Amenhotep III.

The temples of Amun had not been destroyed by Akhenaten – there is no record of any such event.

Tutankhamen started his reign at Memphis and moved to Thebes in year 3.

Tutankhamen was not murdered.

You decide

Conclusion

Conclusion.

"It is good to have an end to journey toward; but it is the journey that matters, in the end" --- **Ernest Hemingway**

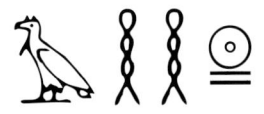

My intention throughout this book has been to present a much more realistic view of events in the late 18th Dynasty Egypt. Some of the things we have been told over the years just did not make sense – 9 year old girls dying in childbirth, carrying her father's child; 70 year old courtiers staging a coup de tat and claiming the throne; an incredibly eccentric Pharaoh ruling the land; no contemporary inscriptions documenting even one voice of dissent when the gods of the land are suddenly abolished – and a homosexual co-regent taking the name of his lover's wife when he chooses his prenomen.

I know that life can be strange, but this stretches the imagination too far.

When examining the rule of Hatshepsut, we looked at the Kings' List, compiled by later dynasties, and we saw that certain names were missing:

Hatshepsut herself, Akhenaten, "Smenkhkare", Tutankhamen and Aye.

Clearly the compilers of the list could see no reason and no place for co-regents, and only recorded the name one Pharaoh. Tuthmoses III was crowned Pharaoh *before* Hatshepsut took power and ruled *after* she had died. So there was no room on the list for Hatshepsut. Where would they have put her? After Tuthmoses II and before Tuthmoses III? Or after Tuthmoses III and before Amenhotep II? Neither placing would have been correct.

Amarna --- the missing evidence

Akhenaten's reign began while Amenhotep III was still Pharaoh. As we now know, there was no Pharaoh Smenkhkare, and Nefertiti was co-regent first to Akhenaten and then to Tutankhamen. Aye had a "caretaker" reign of 2 or 3 years. Horemheb had taken charge of Egypt after the death of Amenhotep III and was ruling *after* the death of Aye. Horemheb nominated Ramses I as his successor, and this Pharaoh was the first of the 19th Dynasty Pharaohs – so understandably Horemheb was incredibly popular after his death. As many people in Egypt had not even noticed Akhenaten or Nefertiti, and as Horemheb was acting as Regent for Tutankhamen, the compilers of the list saw Horemheb as the successor of Amenhotep III.

Horemheb counted the years of his reign from the death of Amenhotep III, and if we step back and look at the whole period of history logically, it all falls into place. A lot of the romanticism and mystery disappears, but I feel that the entire period becomes more interesting. It opens up a whole new range of possibilities and new areas for investigation. The new time-line on page 218 seems very logical and acceptable.

And finally, what of the picture on the front cover? Who is the couple? The man leans on a walking stick and that surely tells it all. 130 walking sticks were found in Tutankhamen's tomb, and that Pharaoh is frequently seen either seated or standing, leaning on his stick. The painted images most likely represent Tutankhamen and his wife, Ankhesenamen.

I hope that you have enjoyed reading the book, and that it has removed some of the fog surrounding earlier explanations. It was not meant to be an exhaustive volume and there is much more to be read. Please take a look at some of the books, publications and web sites that I have recommended. My own web site will be regularly updated I look forward to hearing from you. Thank you for reading.

𓄿𓏭𓏭𓇳

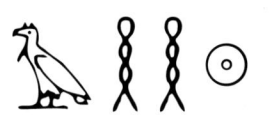

The Revised Timeline

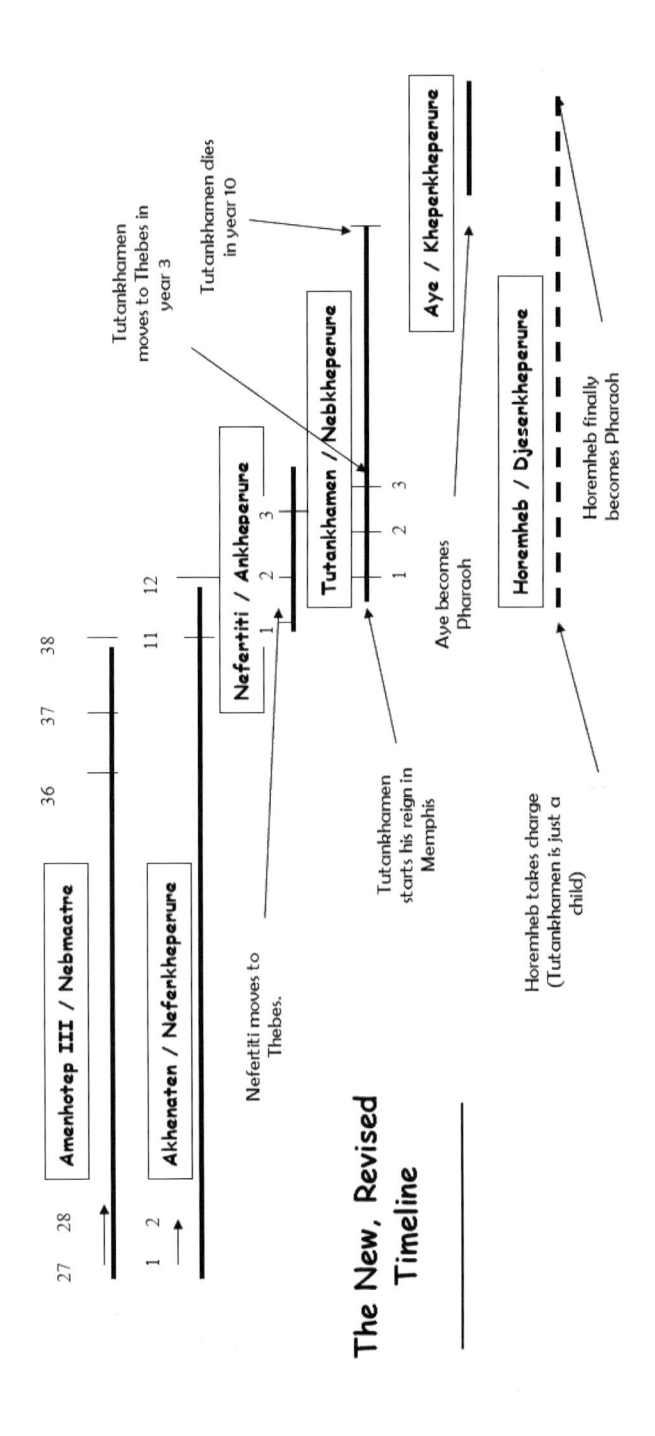

Amenhotep III / Nebmaatre
27 28   36 37 38

Akhenaten / Neferkheperure
1 2 ... 11 12

Nefertiti / Ankhkheperure
1 2 3

Nefertiti moves to Thebes.

Tutankhamen / Nebkheperure
1 2 3

Tutankhamen starts his reign in Memphis

Tutankhamen moves to Thebes in year 3

Tutankhamen dies in year 10

Aye / Kheperkheperure

Aye becomes Pharaoh

Horemheb / Djeserkheperure

Horemheb takes charge (Tutankhamen is just a child)

Horemheb finally becomes Pharaoh

The New, Revised Timeline

Further Reading

Further Reading.

"Reading is to the mind what exercise is to the body." ---
Sir Richard Steele

This is by no means an exhaustive list, but is a range of publications – books, journal articles, magazines, web sites etc. – that I would recommend as relevant to this book.

Books

Aldred, C., 1988 *Akhenaten, King of Egypt.* London. Thames & Hudson Ltd.
Baikie, J., 1926 *The Amarna Age.* London. Black.
de Garis-Davies, N., 1906 *The Rock Tombs of Tel Amarna parts III and IV* London: The Egypt Exploration Fund,
Goedicke, H.,. 1992. *Problems concerning Amenhotep III.* Halgo.
Giles, F J., 1997 *The Amarna Age: Western Asia.* Oxford. Aris & Phillips Ltd
Kitchen, K., 1962 . *Suppiluliuma and the Amarna Pharaohs*. Liverpool. Liverpool Press
Kozloff, ,A., & Bryan, B., 1992 *Royal and Divine Statuary in Egypt's Dazzling Sun: Amenhotep III and his World*, Cleveland Museum of Art and Indiana University Press.
Lichtheim, M., 1980 *Ancient Egyptian Literature, Vol.1,.* Berkley.

Murnane, W J., 1995. *Texts from the Amarna Period in Egypt.* Society of Biblical Literature. Atlanta. Scholars Press.

Moran, W L., 2002 *The Amarna Letters.* London. Baltimore.

Perepelkin, G., 1978 *The Secret of the Golden Coffin* Moscow

Petrie, W M F., 1894 . *Tell El Amarna..* London: Methuen & Co

Petrie, W M F 1896 A *History of Egypt – Part Two.* London: Methuen & Co

Journals and Magazines

Aldred, C., Brief Communications. "Year 12 at Amarna" *Journal of Egyptian Archaeology*

Allen, J.P ."Nefertiti and Smenkh-ka-re", GM 141 (1994), pp.7-17

Dodson, A., "Crown Prince Djhutmose and the Royal Sons of the Eighteenth Dynasty". *Journal of Egyptian Archaeology* 76. p.88

Guterbock, H G., 1956 The Deeds of Suppiluliuma as told by his son, Mursilli II. *Journal of Cuneiform Studies,*

Harrison, R G.,1966 *An Anatomical Examination of the Pharaonic Remains Purported to be Akhenaten*, Journal of Egyptian Archaeology 52

Kemp, B. 2008 *Ancient Egypt* Volume 8 no 6 Issue 48

Newberry P E,. 1928 Akhenaten's Eldest Son-in-Law, Ankhkhneprure, *Journal of Egyptian Archaeology*, 14

Redford, D.,1959. Some observations on Amarna Chronology. *Journal of Egyptian Archaeology* edition 45

Samson, J. J1977 *Egyptian Archaeology* edition 63

Weigall, A., 1922 *Journal of Egyptian Archaeology* 8

Further Reading

Web Sites

www.myamarna.com

http://www.amarnaproject.com/

http://www.nicholasreeves.com/

http://www.touregypt.net/

http://www.ees.ac.uk/

http://www.petrie.ucl.ac.uk/

http://www.museum-tours.com/amarna/

http://www.egyptianmuseum.gov.eg/

http://www.louvre.fr/llv/commun/home.jsp?bmLocale=en

http://www.egyptian-museum-berlin.com/

Index

Abydos 12,16,32
Ahmose 61,63
Ahmose (Pharaoh) 10-12,14,32,35
Ahmose (Queen) 14-15
Ahmose (Son of Ibana) 11
Ahmose Nefertari 13,16
Ahmose-Pen-Nekbet 12
Akhenaten/Amenhotep IV (Pharaoh) 2-4,8-10,13,15,26-43,45-58,60-62,64,66-67,69-76,78-81,83-89,92-95,97-98,100,102-106,108-121,126-128,131-132,135-138,141,145-146,149-151,156-158,160-162,165-171,173-174,180-183,186-187,189-192,194-196.201-204,210,214-215
Akhetaten/Amarna (City of) 9,29-30,40-41-58,60-67,69-76,78,80-81,83,86-87,89,92-93,97-99,104-106,108-109,111-112,115-116,118-121,128,131,160,162,164-165,167,169-174,181-182,186,189-191,195,197,201-205,212
Alpha (chamber in the Royal Tomb) 105,121,183-189,201
Amenmose 15
Amenhotep I (Pharaoh) 12-14,32
Amenhotep II (Pharaoh) 19,20,23,32,41,196,214
Amenhotep III (Pharaoh) 10,23-24,26,32,34-38,41,52-54,58,66,70-72,75,92-93,95-100,102-104,111,114-119,126,128,131,156-160,169-170,173,196,201-202,212,215,220
Amun (god) 13,19,24,26-27,29,31,35-38,40,42,48-52,58,84,96,111,128,132,172,195,203-205,121
Ankhesenpaaten (later amen) 27,31,46,73,186,190,206211,215
Artatama (King of Mitanni) 36
Ashotep (Queen) 10-11
Aye3,12,15,27,29,31,7273,78,81,98,104,111,118,126,128,158,162,173,191,200,205,207,211,214-215

Bek 29,75,83,88-89,113
Beketaten 31,74,100,102,118,202
Book of the Dead 49
Boundary Stelae 13,41-48,137,170,182

Carter, Howard 10,200
Champollion, Jean-François 8,32

Davies, Norman de-Garis 76,136-137,
Davis, Theodore 191-192
D'Avennes, Prisse 133-136,138-143,147-148
Deir-el-Bahri 12,17
Djehuty (Viceroy) 11
Dream Stelae 21,41

Egypt Exploration Society 76,115,136-137

Gamma (chamber in the Royal Tomb) 105,120,184-186
Gardner, Sir Alan 192
Gem-pa-aten 38,40
Gilukhipa 25
Ghurab Papiri 98
Golden Coffin 191,193-195
Gurob Ring 130

Hat 75
Hatiay 75
Hatshepsut 15-19,27,54,164,166,171-172,181,214
Hay, Robert 132-134,138-140,142-149
Hekarnehhe (royal Nurse) 24
Heliopolis 11,22,26,71
Henuttaneb 37
Henry VIII 50-51,202
Horemheb 3,32,51,132,203,205,207,215
Huya 73-75,100-102,106,109,111,114-120,165
Hyksos 10-11,35

Isbka 65
Isis (Queen) 15

Kahmose 10
Karnak 13,17,24,34-35,37,48,51,66,108,157
Khat headdress 17,164
Kiya 31,160,165,197,201-202
Kings Lists 16,32,54,214-215

Lepsius, Karl Richard 133-148
L'Hôte, Nestor 133-134,138-139,147-148
Loret, Victor 23
Luxor 29,35,48,51

Index

Maanakhtef 75
Mahu 69
Malkata 26,104
Marfan's Syndrome 80
May 71
Meketaten 27,47,73,99,102,118,120-121,123,165,182-184,186-187,190
Memphis 9,22,24,26,36,40,70,119,173,195,202,121
Meryre I 62-63
Meryre II 73,75,100,106,109,111,114,116,118,120,132-133,137,140,148-153,165,171
Merytaten 2,27,31,40,44,46-47,112,139,149,162,171,183,186
Merytre-Hatshepsut (Queen) 19
Mitanni 20,31,36-37,95,98,104,106,117,156,159
Mursilli 104,118,209-211
Mut 35
Mutemwia 24,36
Mutnodjme 72-73

Napoleon I (Napoleon Bonaparte) 3,32,191,
Nebetah 37
Neb-nefer 26
Neferkhepere-her-sekhkeper 70
Neferneferuaten-Tasharit 27,108,112,186
Neferneferure 27,112,186
Nefertiti 3,9,26-27,29,31,40,44,46-47,60,72-73,75,78,80-81,84-87,97,100,102,108,110,112,116,119,121,136,150,156-158,160,162-169,171-176,181-183,186,189,191-192,195-197,201-203,209,215,221
Neferure 15-16
Newberry,Percy 137-139,146-147,207
Niqmat (of Ugarti) 189
Nubia 11-13,19,40,201

Osiris 49,111,192

Pa-aten-emheb 72,203
Parennefer 66,70
Pawah 172-173
Pendlebury, John 54,115
Penhesy 64-65
Pentu 63-64

226

Petrie, Flinders 94,130,133-137,140,146,166
Picasso, Pablo 80
Plague 26-27,40,104-105,118-120,123,173,207

Ramose 70,96-97
Ranofer 75,173
Restoration Stelae 51,203-205
Rosetta Stone 8,32

Satiah (Queen) 19
Seqenenre Tao II 10
Setepenre 27,112,186
Shu 47,49,162
Shutarna 25
Sitamun 37
Smenkhkare 2-4,128,130-132,135-137,139-142,148-149,151,153,162,165-167,172,192,195,197,212,214-215
Sobekhotep 23
Sphinx 21-22
Suppiluliuma 104,118,209-210
Sutau 71
Suty 71
Syria 14-15,19-20

Tefnut 162-163
Thebes 9,11,13,24,26-27,29,34-35,38,40-41,43,48-49,52,54,58,60,66,70,73,76,97-98,106,109,111,119,128,131-132,165,169-173,191,195-196,202-203,212
Tiaa (Queen) 20-21
Tiy 10,25,31,36-37,74,95,98-100,102,114-119,156-158,169-170,173,181,190-192,195-196,202,209
Turi (Viceroy of Kush) 13
Tushratta 31,95-96,98,104,117,156-160
Tutankhamen 3,10,31,51,64,84,89,104,120,123,128,131,172-173,186-187,192,195,197,200-212,214,215
Tuthmose 83,87-88,113
Tuthmoses (Prince) 37-38
Tuthmoses I 14,32
Tuthmoses II 15,32,214
Tuthmoses III 15-17,19-20,27,32,54,171,181,214
Tuthmoses IV 17,20-21,23-24,32,35,41,201
Tutu 67-69
Tuya 36-37

Index

Wadjmose 15
Weighing of the Heart 49
Wilkinson, John Gardner 8-9
Wine Jars 53-54, 93, 106, 114

Yuya 36, 37